Princes of Islam

Princes of Islam

David Johnson

Writers Club Press
San Jose New York Lincoln Shanghai

Princes of Islam

All Rights Reserved © 2002 by David E. Johnson

No part of this book may be reproduced or transmitted in any form or by any means, graphic, electronic, or mechanical, including photocopying, recording, taping, or by any information storage retrieval system, without the permission in writing from the publisher.

Writers Club Press
an imprint of iUniverse, Inc.

For information address:
iUniverse, Inc.
5220 S. 16th St., Suite 200
Lincoln, NE 68512
www.iuniverse.com

ISBN: 0-595-21367-7

Printed in the United States of America

Contents

INTRODUCTION vii
Section One the Religion 1
Princes of Islam 3
   Chapter 1 The Hajj 5
   Chapter 2 Back to Reality 14
   Chapter 3 The Birth of Islam 18
   Chapter 4 The Early Years of Islam 23
   Chapter 5 The Islamic Religion And Beliefs 30
Section Two The Historical Princes Go Forth 47
   Chapter 6 The Early Islamic Invaders 49
   Chapter 7 The British Princes Of Islam 54
Section Three Modern Princes go forth to war 59
   Chapter 8 Desert Warlords become Princes. 61
   Chapter 9 Princes on a Sandpile 77
   Chapter 10 The Hashemites Of Jordan 86

Chapter 11 Prince Saddam the Insane 94

Chapter 12 Prince of Damascus 108

Chapter 13 The Ayatollah Princes 118

Chapter 14 The Clown Prince of North Africa 124

Chapter 15 The Chameleon Prince 132

Chapter 16 The Black Prince (who ate his people) 142

Chapter 17 America's Prince Charming 147

Chapter 18 The Prince who lived in a Cave 158

Chapter 19 Islam in America 161

Chapter 20 The American Bird 167

Dictionary of Islamic Terms 173

About the Author 185

Other books by David Earle Johnson 187

INTRODUCTION

The unspeakable atrocities of September 11 will forever remain in the American memory. 9:11 is a day that will "live in infamy" just as much as 12:07 of 1941.

But 9:11 will have to be dealt with and a lesson learned just as the Japanese learned their lesson at Hiroshima and Nagasaki. Had this been the work of one man such as Osama Bin Laden, we could satisfy ourselves by bringing him to death or justice. But it was not one man. It was a system and a so-called "religion." It was and is a system dedicated to the destruction of our way of life and our life itself. That system has to be dealt with now and decisively. There must be no mistaking on the part of the Islamists that America means business. If they perceive America to be a paper tiger, they will strike again and again.

> America has the power to teach Islam a lesson.
> Does America have the determination to do it?

One has to admire the brilliance and the sheer *chutzpah* of Mohammed and his disciples. For a seventh century illiterate, homeless, jobless man to invent a new religion that would ultimately conquer one fifth of the world's population and last a full fourteen centuries was a feat of unparalleled genius. To persuade others to join him in what must have seemed at best a foolhardy enterprise and at worst the prospect of a miserable death, exhibited powers of persuasion never matched by Elmer Gantry and never bettered by Adolph Hitler or Joseph Stalin.

Mohammed, without the aid of the printing press, telephones, mass marketing techniques, the Internet, or even any real transportation, managed to amass an army to conquer Arabia and beyond in his lifetime and found a new religion which would enslave 1.2 billion people in future centuries.

And now, in the twenty-first century, the religion envisaged by this nomadic madman is actually compared to Judaism and Christianity and known as one of the world's "three great religions." The "Book of Mormon" is an obviously phony three-dollar bill printed on cardboard, compared to the monumental work of the Khoran and Hadith. L.Ron Hubbard, the Science Fiction writer turned religion inventor, who gave us the Scientology cult, never dreamed of anything this good. Mohammed and his followers were the very best. They would have been hired by the best tabloid newspaper in America at the drop of a kaffya. "Inquiring minds" have always wanted to know. More than a billion people speak the name of Mohammed several times, every day of the week. Multiplied millions all over the world kneel five times a day and pray toward the ka'bah in Mecca because this man told them they should.

How is this possible?

Mohammed was the first "Prince of Islam." Many have followed. In this volume we shall examine the religion he founded and then take a look at the other "Princes of Islam" who have benefited from the glory of his name.

In order to understand the religion and those who are adherents to it we must read parts of the **Khoran** and the **Hadith** as well as the commentaries on those two collections of teachings by Muslim clerics and philosophers. For me to tell you what I think is just not good enough.

The Islamists are completely persuaded that their way is right and that all other religions are totally wrong. Their mission in life must be to convince all others to convert to Islam, or kill them. Muslim leaders will frequently quote passages from the *Khoran* to their followers to show why they advocate such a bloodthirsty way of bringing about the will of Allah on earth. After seeing a few of these quotations I think you'll agree that they speak for themselves and you will have no need of any convincing from me to see how wild they are. The problem is that they quote a completely different set of verses when speaking to *infidels*. These verses seem to show Islam as a quiet, compassionate, loving religion. Unfortunately our government and our press seem to have accepted the peaceful verses and now refuse to believe the others exist.

This method of misinformation is nowhere better exemplified than in the speeches of Yasir Arafat. He agreed to the conditions of Oslo while with Europeans in Norway, but couldn't get back fast enough to tell the Islamists that he didn't mean any of it. The United States and the Europeans assumed he was sincere. They chose to believe that what he was telling his own people was to "save face." And that he intended to be sincere with us. In fact he was sincere. He was sincerely Islamic, and the Khoran says that believers must not make any agreement with the *infidels*. In the Islamic mind it is absolutely normal to make a promise to an *infidel* and then not keep it because Allah does not even hear such a promise.

Islam is the most wickedly evil power ever unleashed upon the world. Even the Roman Empire for all its sadistic force never came close to the wanton destruction of human life and civilization as this monstrous, inhuman beast. Islam has spread its hateful venom over so many nations in so many parts of the world that every part of the globe suffers to some degree from its results.

Please do not take these facts lightly. Remember the lesson of World War Two. There is little time left to do anything. We must track the beast to its lair and we must render it powerless. But it must be done now.

Dictionary of Islamic Terms

Many of the terms used in the Khoran or by Islamists in today's world are very strange to us, and some translation and explanation are required. I have listed the terms which I feel are the most necessary and useful in the back of this book.

NOTE: The spelling of Arabic words in English depends on something called "transliteration." This is used because Arabic is a Semitic (Middle Eastern) language and uses an alphabet and letters that are different from those we use in English. There are also different sounds, some of which are almost impossible for Americans to master. For instance the word *Khoran* is spelled with the first two letters "kh" or sometimes a "Q" because the first letter in Arabic is pronounced with a catching in the back of the throat almost like the "glottal stop" in German or indeed in Cockney English, but much more difficult. Similarly the last two letters of *Hadith* are "th" because the sound in Arabic for that last letter is something between a "d" and a 't' in English.

Section One

THE RELIGION

PRINCES OF ISLAM

CHAPTER 1

The Hajj

During the course of a few days each year several thousand aircraft arrive in Saudi Arabia from all over the world. The logistics at the terminal of King Abdulaziz International Airport are strained to the limit. Additional air traffic controllers are brought in from other Islamic countries to supplement the Saudi staff. Hundreds of buses, many of them used only once each year, are washed, fueled, and brought to the airport to begin the shuttle service from the airport to Mecca. Long, sleek limousines, chauffeurs at the ready, stand by to ferry the dignitaries. All of the local-born drivers wear the obligatory white robes and headdresses that are a uniform for all Saudis. Pakistani drivers wear a smart tunic and trousers. The brilliant whites and greens of the airport's marble walls gleam in the hot desert sun.

The aircraft begin to arrive, disgorging a torrent of largely unwashed humanity. Many of the aircraft are chartered from state airlines all over the world and refitted to hold more than the usual number of passengers with even less legroom between the seats. Quality is not the important thing here. Quantity is the essential ingredient in bringing such a large army to Mecca for the *Hajj*. Special meal packages have been supplied to conform to Muslim *halelic* rules. The main requirement is that, as in Kosher food, there shall be no pork. The Muslims however do eat shellfish, a divergence from the Kosher rules of their Jewish cousins. As with Kosher meats the *halalic* meats must be properly slaughtered. But the Islamically correct slaughter must include the pronouncement of the name of Allah. There are no bars on these flights and no coffee or tea is served. Muslims do not drink these beverages, at least not around other Muslims.

By the time the flights arrive in Saudi Arabia many of the aircraft have an odor that will take great skill to remove before they go back into regular service. It must be remembered that many of these passengers have never even seen a toilet, particularly the aircraft variety. After all, in many cases the future *hajjis* are from very poor and backward countries. Often the whole village has saved for years to send just one tribal chief to Mecca on his once-in-a-lifetime pilgrimage. The journey for some of these passengers began days ago with a trek to the national airport on foot, by donkey, or in an ancient bus. Many have no suitcase and have never owned one. Their sole possessions for the trip are the clothes they are wearing and a small bundle of banknotes clutched in a grubby hand. One can only imagine what an ordeal this must be for the ones who come from the city where their house boasts not only a toilette, but a shower, to have to sit for eight, ten, even twenty hours among all that stinking humanity.

Finally the aircraft arrives in front of the sparkling terminal building. The prospective *hajjis* are lined up in columns and rows to await their bus into Mecca. Everything is very precise. Everything must be done in the right order. This is a very modern and rich country, rich from oil revenues. The Police are efficient and strict. There is little crime here for two very good reasons. First there are no poor people because everyone benefits from the oil production. Second, if one were tempted to commit a crime, he would consider the very harsh consequences. A thief can lose a hand and a foot on alternate sides as ordered by the Khoran. A rapist would not have the equipment to do it a second time. Death by beheading is a common punishment even for a Saudi Princess who commits adultery. The whole world witnessed this event on television a few years ago. The pilgrims know this in advance. They have no illusions about the Saudi Police. They wait quietly for their transportation. Eventually it comes, a very modern, air conditioned bus. Soon, leaving the airport it climbs up into the brown, lifeless mountains toward Mecca.

Upon arrival in this city of a million people, each group finds its own accommodations. For the rich there are high rise hotels with all the amenities of those in New York and London. For the poor there are designated areas for sleeping on the ground in the open air. There are no classes here. Everyone is an equal on the *hajj*. But some are, as the saying goes, "more equal than others." Two million pilgrims are coming in a wave of jets, plus buses from nearby Islamic countries. Ten thousand come each year from the United States alone, many times that from countries like Indonesia. Two million strangers enter a city that for all but this week in the year has a population of only one million. So for the *hajj* Mecca grows to three times its normal size. The logistics are staggering.

Most of the pilgrims, though exhausted from their journey, cannot wait to begin seeing the sights of this city of their dreams. First stop for most is the central mosque where, in the Great Square, thousands of robed celebrants walk seven times around the ***Ka'bah***. Fifty, seventy-five, even a hundred thousand or more join this counter-clockwise, slow, methodical merry-go-round of joyous humanity. The only sounds are the pilgrims pronouncing the names of Allah and his prophet Mohammed in a buzz of awed whispers, and the swish of white garments as they trail on the stark white, glistening marble of the temple's surface. Some of these people arrived at the airport after as much as twenty hours of flying, yet here they are at three in the morning, before any thought of sleep, ringing the *Ka'bah* with other pilgrims from over one hundred nations.

The *Ka'bah* is to the faithful the very center of the world and the most sacred structure on the face of the planet. It is towards this Ka'bah that Muslims pray five times each day in every part of the world. The Khoran says this was the first house ever built for mankind. It is 30 feet wide and 36 feet long, with a height of 45 feet. The gray stone building stands on a base of pure marble and has no windows. One door leads to the interior and inside the only furnishings are several lamps made of precious metals. On the outside near the door are two stones which are considered sacred. The "stone of good fortune" is built right into the wall at the corner. The other is considered far more important although nobody really seems to know its origin or original purpose. Called the "Black Stone," it has through time broken into several pieces which are held together by a strip of silver. It is not completely black, but has blotches of red and yellow.

As the pilgrims wind their way anti-clockwise around the Ka'bah, they try to catch glimpses of the building and the stones under the black covering or *kiswa.* The origin of the Ka'bah is lost in antiquity. It was worshipped in the days before Mohammed as people of the former polytheistic religions came to Mecca to pray to their gods. The Khoran says that this was the first building ever set up on the earth. But in another place it states that Abraham and Ishmael built it, and this would have been long after Abraham's very advanced city of Ur was built. Others claim that this was the place where Abraham offered Ishmael as a sacrifice to God, but where the angel stopped him from plunging the knife into the boy's heart. Of course the biblical story has Isaac as the potential sacrifice and Mt. Moriah in Jerusalem as the place.

Following the seventh circuit around the Ka'bah, the faithful pilgrims invariably look for a drink of cool water. All around the quadrangled square of the Grand Mosque are stands offering free containers of Zamzam water from the spring of Ishmael. There are officially 10,000 of these containers in this one spot, to make sure none of the pilgrims remains thirsty for long. This is the easy way to be refreshed. But with a little effort most people join the throng waiting to visit the well itself only a few yards away from the Ka'bah. The well is more than one hundred feet deep and said to have been miraculously opened by the angel Jibril (Gabriel) for Hagar and her son Ishmael after they were turned away by Abraham. Remember that Hagar was Sarah's maid and gave birth to Abraham's first son Ishmael. Here we find several hundred basins for ritual washing, and the well itself under a beautiful dome. Pilgrims bend to fill containers of Zamzam water to take home. Some have even brought their future grave clothes to wash them in the sacred waters. Of course if they have forgotten to bring a container they can always order Zamzam over the web when they get home just as Catholics can order Jordan River Water or Holy Land Olive Oil.

On the way back to their various places of lodging, people stop to join long lines to call home, using one of the temporary telephones set up for them by the Saudi Telephone Company. Along the way fires blaze in the campsites and an all pervading aroma of barbecued lamb and goat fills the night air.

Along with the aroma come the voices of Muslims of all nationalities and in almost every tongue known to man. Perhaps the only exception is Hebrew.

At last the airport terminal is closed. No new pilgrims are permitted this year as the *Hajj* gets into high gear. Only Muslims are permitted in Mecca. Papers are checked by roving Police Patrols and at roadblocks. Only the faithful get in touch with Allah and with the Prophet Mohammed.

As the morning of the eighth day of the month dawns, the great crowd begins to stretch and yawn and ebb toward the desert like the waves of an incoming tide. All day long bits and pieces of the two million member sea of humanity plus many of the locals move along the five mile stretch between Mecca and Mina towards the Mina Valley. By noon Mecca will be virtually empty save for the street cleaners and merchants. In Mina one hundred thousand workmen have been busy for weeks setting up 28 thousand fireproof tents to shelter the pilgrims on this next stage of their mission.

Again the Saudi Government has been busy for months working out the logistics of this year's *Hajj*. Learning from the mistakes of past years when hundreds have been trampled to death in stampedes and hundreds of other infected by diseases brought from foreign lands, they have planned the event carefully. Each national contingent has a camp. Each language division has been carefully arranged to fit together and not be separated by another group with another language. With two million people in unfamiliar surroundings it is essential to make finding lost family members as easy as possible. This is a festival for families like nothing else in Islam. In Mosques and Islamic Centers around the world, men and women pray in separate areas, not to be distracted from their worship. Here in Mecca and Mina, where it all started, it is curious to see that they are all together in prayer as in everything else.

The next few days are spent exploring the Pilgrim Way, living like the Bedouin tribesmen from which Mohammed sprang. A few miles to the east is "Mount Mercy" in the valley of Arafat, from which Yasir Arafat borrowed one of his names. The great tent city surrounds the mountain much as the tents of Israel surrounded the Tabernacle in the Wilderness. Prayers are led at noon from atop the mountain. The assembled throng falls on its face as one man. As Jews from all over the world have traveled to Jerusalem for the three pilgrim feasts for three thousand years, so Islamists have traveled to this place for half that time. This is the centerpoint of the Islamic religion. There is little talk here of Jihad. That can wait until they return home to Beirut or Detroit. Here and now for this one week all is peace and brotherhood with fellow Muslims. Nothing else matters. It was from here, from a rocky ledge on Mount Mercy, that Mohammed, so they say, delivered his last sermon to the faithful. It is a sacred place to the followers of Islam.

From here the procession moves back towards Mina stopping along the way to pick up a pocketful of small stones. Later in a symbolic gesture they will hurl their pebbles at some pillars erected along the way which are said to represent Satan.

The next day the *Hajj* ends in the "Feast of Abraham." Hundreds of thousands of lambs and sheep die this morning and are hung on spits over the coals of fires for the noon meal.

In Mecca this evening the successful *Hajjis* bargain with shopkeepers for trinkets and treasures to take home and be admired for years by their friends and families. Gold jewelry, diamonds, sheepskins, pottery, pictures, plaques and prayer mats must be sold tonight or tomorrow. Bookstores boast leather bound volumes of the Khoran and Hadith, teachings by famous Muslim clerics in books and on tape. This is the one week of the year when the merchants of Mecca must make their livelihood for the next year. All night by the light of oil lamps and bare electric bulbs the haggling goes on.

One last act is required by tradition before leaving for the airport or taking the overland route to the outside world. One more set of seven anticlockwise circuits of the *Ka'bah*. One more drink of Zamzam water and the pilgrim is an official *Hajji*. After this he, or she, is considered to have gained the wisdom of a hundred years by their awe-filled friends and relatives back home.

The *Hajj* seems to be a gentle mixture of Baptist Campmeeting and County Fair with two million people dressed in bedsheets.

CHAPTER 2

Back to Reality

George W. Bush said "Islam is Peace." Did he attend a *hajj*? If so this could well have caused him to say "Islam is peace." But the reality is that our President would not have been permitted in Mecca, and that Islam is far from peaceful towards those who are not Muslims.

CNN has done much to cultivate the idea that "Islam is Peace." The network seems to be planning an annual *Hajj* theme by broadcasting from Saudi Arabia each year. Of course the commentators, camera crews and directors are all in—house CNN Muslims. None but Islamists are permitted in Mecca at any time. For this reason we should never expect to see any objective reporting on Islam. If anything adverse to the "party line" ever came to the screen, the "powers that be" in Mecca would shut down the opportunity. What we see is totally one-sided pro-Islamic propaganda. It is also important to note that we never see anything remotely anti-Islamic on any other CNN programming. A network that is "permitted" to film inside Saudi Arabia at the *Hajj*, must remain Islamically correct at all times. In fact we will never see anything remotely critical of Islam on the other channels either. The Islamic world is big business to all TV networks, and they will always err on the side of being pro-Islam in their reporting. To offend Mecca means that their network will be cut off from an essential form of revenue. We must ask ourselves how long our country can survive this constant barrage of propaganda from an enemy that has every intention of destroying our way of life, indeed our life itself. The ironic fact is that Islamists insist that our media are anti-Muslim because they are controlled and owned by Jews. But the exact and emphatic opposite is the case. The American public is beginning to buy this theme of "the Jews control the media" and actually feel sorry for the poor downtrodden Muslims in our country. Of course, if the lie is made big enough and told often enough, everyone will eventually believe it.

By contrast American television networks have never, to my knowledge, broadcast a documentary on any of the biblical festivals from Jerusalem in the same kind of detail as the Hajj. Anything remotely pro-Jewish must always be balanced by opinions from experts who tell us what is wrong with Israel and portray Judaism as a fanatic and obsolete religion. No such experts are permitted to criticize Islam.

One could well imagine that Islam is peace while watching the *Hajj* on television. But the grim reality is that these people may have nothing but peaceful feelings toward each other, but many of them, perhaps the majority of them, have nothing but hate for non-Muslims. Why are the "Princes of Islam" so determined to take the whole world under their domain? The reason is that from their youth they have been taught, "There is no god but Allah, and Mohammed is his prophet." To the fanatically dedicated Muslim, Allah is everything; and everyone who does not submit to Islam must be killed.

CHAPTER 3

The Birth of Islam

Islamic scholars would have us believe that Islam actually started with Adam and Eve and continued through the Islamic prophets, Noah, Moses, and Jesus until the last and greatest prophet, Mohammed. In other words they took all the best of Judaism as found in Torah and Tanach, all the best of Christianity as found in the New Testament, put it all together with ancient pagan moon-god worship, and selected the parts they liked in order to form the Khoran and Hadith.

It is true that much of Mohammed's new religion was based on old religions. People worshipped the moon-god and a large number of idols in the area of Mecca thousands of years ago, and the Grand Mosque is suitably built right on the site of those pagan sacrifices. Fertility gods and goddesses were worshipped in ancient times, and sacrifices were made to them to produce both crops and children. The ancient pagans prayed towards the *ka'bah* several times each day and made an annual pilgrimage to the spot just as their followers the Islamists do today. The moon-god origins of Islam are proudly displayed on the flags of many Islamic nations, and the crescent moon stands atop mosques and on the emblem of the Muslim version of the Red Cross, the "Red Crescent Society." True, most Muslims have no idea that they are worshipping the ancient moon-god. His name is Allah and in their eyes he is the god of paradise who created the world.

The Pope declared several times during the past few years that "God and Allah are the same." He also requested that Catholics fast on the last day of Ramadan 2001 "in solidarity with Muslims." It's a good thing Catholics do not still believe in the infallibility of the Pope. It almost sounds as if he is saying that Islam and Catholicism are one.

Mohammed did not write the Khoran – not a word of it. He was illiterate. This makes it almost more amazing that the writings could have existed and lasted through so many centuries. It was written by scribes and disciples who might well have added their own thoughts, since Mohammed was unable to check what was written. Also much of it was added in the centuries following Mohammed's death, so we do not know for sure how much of the Khoran really came from the lips of "the Prophet."

One could almost imagine a skit on the "Monty Python Show" where Mohammed's disciples read parts of the Tanach and parts of the New Testament to him and he decides which parts to include in his new book, "The Khoran." A committee would have decided which of the Hebrew Prophets would have plastic surgery and take advantage of the "Federal Witness Program" to be re-incarnated as Islamic prophets. They would all agree on Jesus because he was very popular all over the Middle East at the time. Angry disciples would add verses calling for war against the neighboring countries. Henpecked husbands would get back at their wives by including admonitions to beat them and divorce them. Sexual predators would include the right to rape all non-Muslim women, and lusty young men would demand several wives. Paradise was essential. You couldn't expect to attract followers to a religion that didn't offer something better than they had here on earth. Hell was also necessary because there had to be a good reason to want to follow Allah and his prophet Mohammed.

Of course, as with all new religions, Islam took on a life of its own after the original authors died. New prophets and teachers have been falling all over each other to add their wisdom to that of the Prophet for more than 1300 years. All that was required of new expounders of Islam was that they should spend time learning from the great teachers and then found their own little group of disciples. After this they were able to publish papers on their own theories and add to their clan anyone who believed them. It reminds me of Ian Fleming who wrote the original James Bond books in the sixties. After he died several authors who were ardent aficionados of the James Bond tradition were able to write new James Bond adventures and turn some of them into movies. All they had to do was to take the basic features of Bond, – James Bond and weave a new story around the character. It really wasn't difficult because Fleming's characters, Bond, "M", Miss Moneypenny, and the agents of

SMERSH, were all so shallow and predictable that the new Bond fitted perfectly into almost any plot that was far-fetched and dealt with a romantic, tuxedoed Rambo with super spy weapons at his disposal. After all Mohammed's original group of script writers based all their "teachings" on the Tanach and the New Testament with their own sadistic twists. The new experts needed only to continue that line of reasoning to get a crowd to follow them.

CHAPTER 4

The Early Years of Islam

Mohammed was supposedly commissioned by Allah as a prophet, in a cave in the year 610 and he immediately began to have visions and make plans. His new religion, even though built so much on other popular religions, was not well received by the citizens of Mecca. They were for the most part worshippers of multiple gods but there was also a fairly substantial Jewish community and some Meccans had converted to Judaism. The Jews ran flourishing markets in Mecca, Medina, and other nearby towns, offering the goods that came in on the caravans from Yemen and Africa in the south and from Damascus, Europe, and India in the north, as well as locally made merchandise and crops. Mecca was set apart as a city of refuge where all could flee from the conflicts of the surrounding tribes. In Mecca the people worshipped at the pagan shrines and engaged in commerce with the surrounding towns and encampments. Regular convoys of caravans moved back and forth between Mecca and the civilizations to the north and south, and Mecca was declared a *Harram*, or sanctuary city, where no war or strife was permitted.

Mohammed's wife and benefactor Khadija died in 619, and after a suitable period of mourning he went in search of other wives. When his announced prophethood was rudely rebuffed by the citizens of Mecca, the Prophet went in 622 upon invitation to live in Medina (then known as Yatrib) with some of his converts. His journey or *hijrah* to Medina is held as a sacred date by the followers and the Muslim calendar begins with this date. These faithful early Muslims gave the Prophet a piece of land large enough to build houses in a compound for each of his wives.

At first they lived on donations offered by the faithful Meccans and the profits from market stalls run by some of his followers in the local Jewish bazaar. But eventually Mohammed realized that he must make some effort to earn an honest living himself, so he went into the only business he really understood. In 623 he organized and led three hijackings of caravans passing along the trade route from Syria to Mecca. Unfortunately all three raids failed, for if they had been successful he might have given up the idea of becoming a Prophet and pursued a life of honest crime, which was a way of life to the Arabs. In 624 he was at last successful and his little band brought home a fine haul in the spirit of Robin Hood, robbing the rich to aid the poor Islamists.

During these first few years Mohammed had been very close to the Jewish community, protecting them and cultivating their friendships because he thought at first that they would be receptive to his claim to be a prophet. They had had more experience with prophets than any other culture, and he probably thought they would accept him as just another in the line. When they rebuffed him even more forcefully than had the pagan citizens of Mecca, he finally gave up on the Jews and from then on they were his number one enemy.

Mohammed justified being a brigand by claiming that he was merely doing the will of Allah. After all, if these people did not convert to his religion they didn't deserve to have anything. He continued to hijack the caravans on the nearby trade route but by now the citizens of Mecca were enraged enough at his audacity that they determined to teach him a lesson he would never forget. Mohammed's raiding party of just over three hundred men was met, on March 15, 624, by a force of about eight hundred Meccans in addition to the small party of troops attached to the caravan. Thus, outnumbered nearly three to one Mohammed's Muslims met the challenge of the "Battle of Badr" which has since been defined as a major turning point in the Prophet's career.

Forty-five Meccans were killed including their general and several of his officers, and seventy were taken prisoner. Muslim casualties were only fourteen dead, and a few wounded.

Mohammed announced that this great victory for Islam proved that he was a prophet sent from Allah. Mohammed's force returned to Medina where he promptly executed some of those who opposed him and made fun of his new religion, and expelled all of the Jews from the city. From here on nobody in Medina would dare to oppose him and he thought the same would apply to those in Mecca. He continued to attack everyone within striking distance with his murderous band. No caravan was safe and no Arab village or encampment was spared. His army murdered, raped, and stole everything they could carry back to Medina including any women to whom they took a fancy. It was good to work for Mohammed. His new religion offered more than they could ever have dreamed of: riches for which they did not have to work, all the women they could possibly want, and paradise too.

Abu Sufyan, the man whose caravan Mohammed had attacked at Badr was determined to wipe out the Muslims in retaliation, but it took him a year and six days to gather an army of three thousand men to attack the Islamists. He came upon Mohammed's men in Medina on March 21, 625, as they were working in the grain fields of the oasis. Mohammed ordered his men to retreat to a series of fortified buildings, but the Meccans, by burning the Muslem's crops forced them to come out and fight.

On the following night Mohammed took a thousand men and climbed a hill called Mt. Uhud behind the Meccan camp so that the enemy was now surrounded. The Islamic army fought off the foot soldiers, and the horsemen were unable to reach them in their position on the hill. The Meccans decided to withdraw and return home with neither army having won the battle.

It was just over two years before the Meccans tried once more to wipe out Mohammed's forces. In April 627 the intrepid Abu Sufyan came with a force of now 10,000 men; more than three times the size of his last army. But Mohammed had taken the intervening two years to build up his defenses, including digging a great ditch past which he hoped his enemy could come. It did indeed prove too much for the Meccan horsemen who were the mainstay of Abu Sufyan's armed force, and they were forced to withdraw once more.

It was now time for Mohammed to take out his anger again on the Jews. It seems that this was his idea of relaxation after a battle. The Islamic history books say he "expelled" the Jewish community of Banu

Quraiza. In fact, he attacked the small and almost defenseless group and forced them to surrender. He then executed all of the men and sold the women and children as slaves only after his men had finished using them.

In 629 Mohammed made a pilgrimage to Mecca and then returned the next January with an army of 10,000 men. Abu Sufyan and the elders of the city went out to meet Mohammed some distance from the city and formally surrendered to him. Under the terms of the surrender there was almost no fighting and a total of only thirty people died. Most of the city converted to Islam. Spending two or three weeks in the city to set up his administration Mohammed gave his first order: that all of the idols in the *Ka-bah* and all local shrines should be destroyed.

Mohammed led several more wars during the next two years and made one final pilgrimage to Mecca in 632. Two months later he became ill in Medina and died there on June 8, 632.

Having briefly studied the life of the prophet of Islam and witnessed the violence he taught his followers, can anyone wonder that the Muslims are so wickedly violent today? After 14 centuries of murder and destruction and with a current army of 1.2 billion troops ready to give their lives for Islam the leaders of Allah's army are almost ready to strike. And strike they will, when they are ready.

Would somebody please explain this to our President. His advisors have told him that -

"Islam means Peace."
Nothing could be much further from the truth.

It is frightening to compare Chamberlain's statement "Peace in our time" as he returned from meeting Hitler on September 30, 1938, to George Bush's assertion that "Islam is peace" in 2001.

Just eleven months after Chamberlain's statement, the World was in full-scale war against the Nazis. How long will it be before we are faced with the same reality, but on a far grander scale?

CHAPTER 5

The Islamic Religion And Beliefs

Muslims believe that Allah revealed the Koran to Mohammed in visions. Some of the beliefs are similar in many ways to Judaism and Christianity. But why wouldn't they be? Mohammed and his contemporaries had been immersed in both religions since they were children. They knew the Bible stories. So when Mohammed had his visions, they were often inspired by stories and teachings he had heard. In other words those visions attributed to Mohammed were pure fiction built on a thin foundation of fact.

Whenever man sets out to found a new religion, he builds into it those things that he wants. I know a lady who wants a religion in which the sermons are short and interesting without much emphasis on God and with not too much reference to the Bible. The church must have individual seats, not pews, so that one can be independent. Abortion must be permitted in this religion because she once had one and would not want to have to repent. She has visited a number of churches and never found the perfect one. In one instance there was no place in the chair in front of her to place her hymn book which meant that she had to balance the book on her knee for the rest of the service. Such an inconvenient religion was not for her.

In order to keep believers focused on their new religion, Mohammed devised a set of very stringent laws, which included praying toward Mecca five times a day, ritual washing before prayer, and recitation of the Koran. This total immersion in the religion left little time for thinking of anything else and kept students in line very well.

Every believer must, at least once in his life, say
"There is no God but Allah and Mohammed is his prophet."

The Moslem religion teaches that the belief of the majority is truth. Therefore the religion may change at any time. It may also be different in each country.

The Moslem prayer hall or Mosque must contain
A) A raised platform.
B) Prayer rugs.
C) A pulpit.
D) A prayer niche facing Mecca.

    The mention of prayer rugs reminds me of a story told to me by a Christian Arab friend in Jerusalem many years ago. The story goes that during the time when Jerusalem was under the control of Jordan, a few of the faithful who had plenty of money and liked to travel used to come to the city to pray at the Mosque of Al Aksar, which is considered the third most holy shrine of Islam, and the Mosque of Omar. Being rich with oil money they brought with them their own richly embroidered prayer rugs. On their return home they frequently sold the rugs to local merchants to save the bother of carrying them back. After observing this ritual for some time, my friend came up with the idea of exporting the used rugs to England where they could be sold for far more than in Jerusalem. So he began making fairly frequent trips to London with suitcases crammed with prayer rugs.
    The British Customs Service is not known for employing country bumpkins, and it wasn't long before they caught on to this new industry. A new rule was soon instituted that Muslims could bring in a few prayer rugs for their own personal use while in Britain, but not to sell. On one occasion when my friend was asked to open his suitcases, the Customs Inspector looked dubiously at him and asked, "Are you a Muslim, Sir?" At this point my friend looked at his watch and asked, " Quickly, which way is East?" He then grabbed one of the rugs, threw it on the floor, and stretched out on it in the direction of Mecca intoning the Muslim prayer *"Allahu Achba"* (Allah is Greater).

ISLAMIC BELIEFS

About the meaning of Islam

Islam means, quite simply "submission." It means that those who do not willingly submit to the teachings of Mohammed must be forced to submit. If they do not submit by force, they must die. George W. Bush told the world on September 12th 2001 that "Islam is Peace." He has not retracted that erroneous statement in spite of so much proof that the opposite is true. Islam, in fact, means total war between the Islamists and the rest of the world. Any Muslim knows this. If our government does not soon learn the truth about Islam and begin to fight the worldwide *Islamic Jihad,* we cannot win against them. They are totally dedicated to our destruction and their strength and determination are growing daily.

About Christians

Christians are bound for Hell for two major reasons. First they do not accept Mohammed as the last and greatest Prophet of Allah. Second, they believe that Jesus is the son of God, which makes them heretics. There is no god but Allah and Mohammed is his prophet. Allah is one and cannot possibly have a son. When Jesus (the Islamic Prophet) referred to himself as "son of God" he was using the term in the sense that we are all sons and daughters of God, since we were all created by Him.

About Jews

Jews are also guilty of heresy because they do not believe in Mohammed or in Allah. The ways of Allah were first made known to the Jews, but they refused to submit to Islam. Jesus and Mohammed were sent by Allah to bring them back into the way. Since they refused to listen to either of the final two prophets they were consigned to Hell unless they repent and convert to Islam.

About Women

Women were created to serve men and produce children. Those who do not pray or do not respect their husbands must be punished by being beaten. Those who commit adultery or profane the name of Allah are to be killed.

About how Jews or Christians can be saved from Hell?

They can convert to Islam and, while they will be somewhat second class citizens, they will be redeemed from the fires of Hell. If they do not convert to Islam they must at least acknowledge Mohammed as the prophet and pay a tax to the Islamic authority to be allowed to live at all. If they fail to do these things, they must be killed.

About Muslims who make friends with Jews and Christians.

Shaykh (Sheik) Muhammad ibn Salih al-Uthaymeen explains that in Islamic teaching Jews and Christians are Kuffaars (Kafirs), disbelievers. All Kuffars will go to hell. "Those who disbelieve among the People of the Book and the idolaters will abide in the Fire of Hell." (al-Bayyinah 98:6). This teaching is given over and over again in the Hadith. Any Muslim who rejects the idea that Jews and Christians are unbelievers is himself an unbeliever because he is in fact denying what Allah himself has said. Denying what Allah has said is blasphemy. Blasphemy against Allah is worthy of death. This means that any Islamist who does not condemn Christians and Jews is himself a disbeliever.

The sheik complains that Christians and Jews wish Muslims to compromise in religion out of courtesy so that they would, in turn compromise.(al-Qualam 68:9). But these people (Christians and Jews) are the inhabitants of hell-fire.

In America's race to become "Islamically correct," our government and our news media have done everything they can think of to compromise to satisfy the Princes of Islam. Nothing has been held back. We have even allowed the priests of Islam to pray to their false god in the Senate and the House of Representatives. They have been made honored guests in the White House for Ramadan by the Clintons and now, unbelievably, by the Bush family. We have totally compromised everything America stands for. And the Islamists have made no compromise whatsoever. They are winning on every front because America does not understand who we are up against.

About making agreements with Infidels

No agreement with an Infidel or non-Muslim nation, or government is valid. Allah does not witness such an agreement so it may be broken without a second thought.

About Defection from Islam

Islamic law is very harsh when it comes to those who defect. Anyone who accepts Islam once and then rejects it is not fit to live. He is given sixty days in which to repent and then the death sentence is carried out. He is worse than an infidel.

Although civil courts in Islamic countries are bound to carry out such death sentences, they rarely do. International outrage usually brings sanity to these cases and sentences are commuted. However this does not mean that people are not put do death for apostasy in rural towns and even major cities. Local Imams issue fatwahs and mobs of Islamic fanatics carry them out.

About Islamic Law

Muslims believe that Islamic law is based on the Khoran and that as such it is the perfect will of Allah. Allah is kind and merciful to those who repent but administers devastating punishment to those who refuse to repent of sins against the Khoran. Islamic Law is the only valid law in the world. From this brief explanation it becomes clear to the western mind why the Islamists tried, immediately after September 11, to get the West to agree to Bin Laden being tried in an Islamic Court. The fact is that no Islamic court in the world could possibly find him guilty of anything. He carried out Islamic law perfectly in administering punishment to the evildoers. The West must learn that the Islamic mind does not operate in Western concepts. They do not recognize the United States Supreme Court or our government because they are not Islamic. The World Court in The Hague means nothing to them. President Bush, Prime Minister Blair, and other western leaders just don't understand that Islam considers them fools to be used for Islam's purposes and then discarded and killed when the time comes. The Islamic logic operates on the laws of the Khoran as interpreted by Islamic scholars and no other laws are legitimate in their eyes. So while the West has done everything they can think of to please our Islamic "allies" in the war against terrorism, the Islamists are laughing at us and waiting for the final battle in which they will inevitably conquer us. Dinners in the White House and Islamic prayers in Congress are but one more step towards the final conquest.

The main seat of Islamic learning is Azhar University in Cairo. There is nothing quite like this in the Western world because our laws are based upon totally different structures. In the United States our laws are rooted in English Common Law, a code which has evolved over the centuries to suit civilization's need for equity. As a new situation arises, new laws are hammered out in our Congress, the legislative assembly of our government and of the various state governments. The laws are then interpreted by the judiciary and the highest authority of the judiciary is our Supreme Court. There really are no new laws in Islam. Everything was covered in the Khoran and the basic principles can never be changed. The Doctors of Islamic Law at Azhar University are the interpreters of Islamic Law and hand down final decisions much as our Supreme Court does. This does not mean that a Sheik or Imam in some obscure town is forced to abide by those interpretations. Indeed there are frequent disputes by individuals and groups, which often lead to war. For instance when Iraqi forces invaded Kuwait at the start of the Gulf War, this was clearly against Islamic Law. The law encourages aggression against infidels, but not against fellow Islamists.

It should also be noted that other Islamic entities frequently issue rulings. For instance, as one might imagine there is a seat of learning in Mecca which may not always agree on the interpretations of Azham University. Also the civil authorities in some Islamic countries occasionally pass their own sets of laws, generally complementing those of the religious communities. For instance in 1977, the Egyptian Government announced that the State Assembly had approved a bill to set the penalty for apostasy (leaving Islam).

"The apostate who intentionally relinquishes Islam by explicit declaration or decisive deed must be put to death. Apostasy is established by one confirmation or by the testimony of two men. The apostate is forbidden to administer his properties. He will be given 30 days to repent before the execution of the sentence of death. But if one converted to Christianity was 10-14 years old, he will only be scourged fifty times."

The bill was never put into practice in Egypt because of the world outcry against it. But while the law was officially never enacted the fact is that it is carried out by the religious authorities and people are executed for becoming Christians.

The legislators of Azhar issued a document of Islamically Legal Punishments and sent it to all mosques in the West. Among other punishments, thieves are to have alternate hands and feet amputated and women accused of adultery are to be executed. Although these laws reached the United States it is doubtful that they have as yet been carried out here. That is something which must wait until the Islamists are stronger in the United States. Even so there is nothing to stop an individual Muslim or a group of Muslims carrying out such sentences, and we know that in some cases it has been done in America.

About Jesus

This is going to be the shocker for most Christians. Muslims absolutely believe in Jesus whom they call Issa. They usually refer to him as Issa bin Marium, or Jesus son of Mary to avoid confusion with other Issas. They believe he was a real person and a Jewish prophet and teacher. They believe that he will return one day soon to kill the Dajjal, anti-Christ. In fact they say the Muslim Nation has more right to Jesus than any other because Jesus was a Messenger of Allah just as Mohammed was. Jesus was the last of a line of prophets who came to herald the arrival of the one great prophet and Messenger of Allah, Mohammed. Since in their view both the Jews and the Christians left the faith of Abraham, the Muslims are the only ones worthy of Jesus. In fact according to the Islamists, Jesus himself rejects all Christians because they reject the greater prophet Mohammed.

In Muslim theology one must believe in all the prophets, and if one believes in one of them then he automatically believes in all because they all brought the same message from Allah. Thus Noah, Elijah, Jesus, and Mohammed all speak the same word. If a person believes the message of Jesus or indeed of Elijah he must believe also in Mohammed's teaching. If he refutes the teachings of Mohammed he is a double infidel. One who knows nothing of Allah has less blame than one who accepts Abraham or Jesus but refuses the greatest prophet of all. In the Khoran Surat ash-Shu'arah 26:105 we read that *"Nuh's people disbelieved the messengers."* Nuh is the Islamic form of Noah and the passage as written in the Khoran intimates that there were more messengers than Noah alone who were disbelieved. The explanation of this is that in disbelieving Noah they also disbelieved both Jesus and Mohammed even though these two messengers were yet to come many centuries later. All of God's prophets are related and one must believe them all in order to make peace with Allah and hear his complete word to mankind.

According to Muslim theologian Yahya Adel Ibrahim, Muslims even believe in the virgin birth of Jesus. Islam has no quarrel with Jesus because they simply make him equal with the other Muslim prophets and just a little less than Mohammed. The only part of the New Testament they don't believe is that Jesus died on the cross. According to Islam he nearly died and then went to heaven to wait for his next assignment.

Muslims revere Jesus' mother Miriam (Remember of course that the name Mary was only the Roman translation of the Jewish name Miriam), as one of only four perfect women in history. Muslim teacher Rassol ul Allah states, "Many men have reached completion (in their relationship with Allah) such as the many thousands of prophets. Yet, only four women have reached completion: Mirium bint Imran, Asiya the wife of Pharoah, Kadijah bint Khuwaylid and Fatima bint Mohammed.

Muslims revere Miriam highly and say that the angels appeared to her and said, "O Marium! Verily, Allah has chosen you, purified you (from disbelief and sin) and chosen you from among all women. O Marium submit yourself with obedience to your Lord (Allah) and prostrate yourself and bow down." Ali-Imran 3:42-43.

As Islam has it, Miriam left her family and went to a place that faced East where she placed a tent around herself and met the angel Jibreel (Gabriel) who explained how Allah would form a baby in her womb. "How can this be possible," she asks "since I have not had intercourse with a man?" Gabriel tells her that is easy for Allah and Allah wants to make her son as a sign for mankind of mercy from Allah. Notice that in order to conceive Jesus, Miriam has to go to a place facing east, that is toward Mecca (Bethlehem).

Muslims are expecting Jesus to return soon to dispense justice upon earth according to the laws of Mohammed and to kill the Dajjal, the one eyed anti-Messiah. His "Second Coming" will be heralded by great Muslim victories over the evil Jewish and Christian nations. They further believe that all of the "People of the Book" will believe in Jesus, son of Mary, before Jesus' death. Some Muslims wonder why Jesus will have such a prominent part in the End of the World as he, not Mohammed, descends from Heaven to kill the anti-Christ. The answer is that Jesus will be acting as the servant of Mohammed and will bring with him Mohammed's laws to dispense justice in the name of Allah.

We must remember that Mohammed's followers wrote the Khoran and the Hadith starting in the early seventh century. The texts of both the Tannach and the New Testament were well known by this time. It was not too difficult to write a book that would include the best parts of each but would also change God to Allah, and thrust forward the teachings and supposed exploits of Mohammed. It was rather like a screenwriter re-working a novel to attract a television audience and come to exciting cliffhangers before each commercial break. For instance here's a quotation from Jesus (Islamic version). Allah says "Then when Issa came to know their disbelief he said 'Who will be my helpers in Allah's cause?' The disciples said: 'We are the helpers of Allah; we believe in Allah, and bear witness that we are Muslims." Ali-'Imran (3:52).

About the Future

Muslims believe that the world will soon be generally converted to Islam and that those who have not converted will be under Muslim rule and Islamic Law. It will then be time for Issa (Jesus) to return to vanquish the devil and judge mankind.

This belief makes it clear why Islamists feel compelled to wage a Holy War against America and Israel. These are the only two countries still standing against the worldwide Muslim takeover. It is their duty to Allah to bring about total Islamic rule as soon as they have enough weapons to bring it about.

About Muslim World Domination

Muslim leaders in the United States have vehemently denied that the concept of *Jihad* or Holy War exists. Our President and members of his cabinet have apparently fallen for this lie because they speak of the Peaceful Religion of Islam. But the facts are quite the opposite. The Khoran and respected (if that is the right word) Islamic Scholars throughout the world write that the Holy War is the very essence of Islamic teaching.

Islamic literature shows that Muhammed not only embraced this doctrine, but conceived it, and commanded his followers to embrace it. Here is a direct quote from the "prophet."

"I have been ordered by Allah to fight with people until they bear testimony to the fact that there is no god but Allah and that Mohammed is his messenger, and that they establish prayer and pay Zakat. If they do it their blood and their property are safe from me." Bukhari Vol 1, page 13.

This doctrine is not only embraced by all the leading Islamic Scholars of today. It is taught by them as essential fact. The statement clearly shows that Mohammed taught his followers to kill anyone who did not bow to him and his religion. All Arabs must convert without any qualification or die. Christians and Jews must either convert or at least acknowledge Mohammed's teachings and pay him a tax, or they will be killed.

The scholars of Azhar University in Cairo are considered to be a major authority in the Islamic world of today, and Dr. Muhammad Sa'id Ramadan al-Buti is foremost among them as a writer and lecturer on Islamic Law. In his book "Jurisprudence in Mohammed's Biography," Dr. al-Buti states.

"The Holy War, as it is known in Islamic Jurisprudence, is basically an offensive war. This is the duty of Muslims in every age when the needed military power becomes available to them. This is the phase in which the meaning of Holy War has taken its final form. Thus the apostle of god said: I was commanded to fight the people until they believe in god and his message...."

This is the undeniable attitude of all the leading Islamic Scholars, teachers, and Imams throughout the world. There is no possibility of a dedicated Muslim thinking other than that all infidels must be forced to accept Islam in one way or another, or they must die.

Note the words *"This is the duty of Muslims in every age when the needed military power becomes available to them."*

During the past twenty years every major arms producing nation has been selling as much military hardware as it possibly can to all of the Islamic States. The United States is guilty of arming them with aircraft, ships, and conventional weapons including small missiles. Other countries, notably China, have provided long range rockets capable of delivering nuclear and biological warheads to our cities.

Go back once more and look at the basic Islamic policy statement. **"This is the duty of Muslims in every age when the needed military power becomes available to them."**

What is *"the duty?"* To make war upon all who do not believe in Allah and his prophet.

Can we rely upon President Bush's statement that "Islam means Peace?" Or should we believe the Islamists themselves. In my opinion we would be very foolish to ignore them. There are far more of them than of us. They have the nuclear weapons. They have never before swerved from their objective and will not now as they near what they believe is the end of the world. They will take over the world if we do not act now and act decisively.

The Five Pillars of Islam

Shahaadah

Declare faith in Allah as the one god and Mohammed as his prophet.

Zakat

Giving of Alms. One should give just a little above what is required by Shariah law, to be on the safe side.

Hajj

The pilgrimage to Mecca should be undertaken at least once in a lifetime, more often if possible.

Salat

The faithful must pray five times a day facing the Ka'bah in Mecca. Before praying they must wash ritually.

Sawm

Fasting during the month of Ramadan from morning to evening. An evening meal is permitted.

Section Two

The Historical Princes Go Forth

CHAPTER 6

The Early Islamic Invaders

The Islamists have managed to persuade many in our government that Islam is nothing but a peaceful religion. President Bush's now infamous pronouncement that "Islam is Peace," makes it very clear that the monumental deception has worked perfectly. One has only to make a cursory inspection of history, however, to realize how big a lie that really is.

In 586 at the age of fifteen Mohammed participated in the war of Fijar. Eight years later he became manager of the business owned by a lady by the name of Khadijah and persuaded her to marry him the following year. In 610 he claimed his first revelation at the age of 39 and soon began attacking the tribes and cities around him. Mohammed's first major battle was at Badr in 624, and between then and his death in 632 at the age of 61 he had been involved in eleven major battles. Eleven major battles in the space of just eight years. I would have trouble in describing this as a peaceful religion.

But the Islamic commanders and leaders were only beginning to warm up by the time of their "Prophet's" death. During the next ten years they attacked forty-nine cities, towns, and countries. The slaughter went on unabated for hundreds of years. In fact within one hundred years of the death of Mohammed, his followers had enslaved the Arabian Peninsula, Egypt, North Africa, Spain, Portugal, Southern France, the Mediterranean Islands, Italy, Greece, Turkey, Afghanistan, part of India and Pakistan, Iran, and Southern Russia. Obviously Mr. Bush knows nothing of their history if he thinks "Islam means Peace."

The next one thousand years were spent in consolidating the conquests of the early leaders and expanding just a little. But mostly the various Caliphs, Sultans, Princes, and WarLords who had grabbed their part of the spoils fought among themselves.

Perhaps the best known warrior of this period was Salah ad-din Yusuf or Saladin as he is known in the West. Born in Tikrit, Iraq (also the birthplace of Saddam Hussein), in 1138, of Kurdish parents he joined the Syrian Army at age 14. By 1169 he had distinguished himself as a fighter to the point of being made commander-in-chief of the

Syrian Army at age 31. He fought against the Crusaders, but also against other Muslim leaders, until on July 4th 1187 he defeated the Christian armies at the Horns of Hittin in Galilee and went on to capture Jerusalem, a Crusader stronghold, a few months later. Two years later the Pope's forces raised another Crusade and with a land and sea invasion forced Saladin to give up the coastal plain in exchange for allowing him to keep Jerusalem in Islamic hands.

Today one can still see the monuments to Saladin in Jerusalem, and a street in East Jerusalem is named for him. But his enduring memory among westerners is surely the Arab Prince, like Rudolph Valentino, on a white horse.

Despite a brief time here and there when a leader such as Saladin rose to conquer and re-conquer cities from invading Europeans, most of the action in the first thousand years of Islam was between warring petty lords who declared their own empires.

The results were quite comical by modern standards as seen by the names of some of the empires. There were the Khiljis Empire; the Churgill Empire; the Samudra Pasai Empire; the Sabadaran Empire; the Maranids Empire; the Tughluqs Empire; the Ottoman Turkish Empire; the Muzaffarids Empire; the Golden Horde Empire; the Bahmanids Empire; the Black Sheep Empire, the White Sheep Empire, Amir Temurs Empire; the Jalayar Empire, the Burji Mamluks Empire, and the Timuids Empire to mention a few of the larger ones.

When the Muslims were not cutting the throats of the infidels, they were cutting each other's throats. And the sad fact is that they are still doing the very same things today, but on a much wider scale.

In 1528 the Ottoman armies took Buda in Hungary, half of what today is known as Budapest. In 1529 they laid siege to Vienna, but were not able to accomplish their goal. In 1550 Islam spread with invading armies to Sumartra, Java, the Molucca Islands, and Borneo, all island states of Indonesia.

All of these new outposts of Islam were acquired, and the accompanying consolidation of old empires was accomplished, by the petty princes of Islam who warred against each other as well as the infidels. There has never been collaboration on any grand scale, and no real central leadership since the time of Mohammed. But this should not give reason for us to breathe more easily. Look at what they have accomplished because all of their factions and empires have one congealing factor. They all believe that Allah is God and that it is his will for them to subjugate the entire world, converting by force of arms.

CHAPTER 7

The British Princes Of Islam

At first the title of this chapter might seem strange and inappropriate. But without the help of two British military commanders it is possible that the Islamists of today would not be in the commanding position they are.

The Muslims were used to fighting among themselves and controlling peoples who were already beaten and subservient. If they were to fight against modern armies with European military strategists, they would have to learn from men who had been trained in European War Colleges. There were two such men and they would in time train some of the Islamic armies and prepare them to form their own general staffs and war colleges. They were Thomas Edward Lawrence and John Baggot Glubb. They were unrepentant Arabists and were indeed "Princes of Islam."

T.E.Lawrence, known to his friends as Ned, was born in Wales in 1888. His father was Sir Thomas Chapman and his mother was the former family governess Sarah Junner. Having eloped and neglected to get married officially, they chose the name of Lawrence and it was under this name that their five sons, including Ned, were brought into the world.

Ned did very well at school. In fact he was a brilliant student at Oxford and, following a walking tour of Syria and Israel, offered a thesis on Crusader Castles. Later he spent some time on an archeological dig in Iraq during which he learned to deal with the Arabs using his powers of reason, rather than the power of military might. During the First World War he was posted to Cairo with British Military Intelligence and became an expert in Arab affairs as well as an Arabphile.

Turkey had been the ruling power throughout the Arab lands while the Arabs were little more than a collection of wandering desert tribes. The Germans had taken the Turkish side during the war, while the British cultivated the Arabs, as once again factions among the Islamists opposed one another in the struggle for power.

After the War, Lawrence promoted the cause of Arab independence while France and Britain sought to divide the territory between them. France grabbed Syria and Lebanon while Britain took Palestine and Iraq as virtually part of their Empires. Lawrence, who had previously been unknown back home in England, now began writing and lecturing and, with the help of American reporter Lowell Thomas, was soon a veritable cult figure known as "Lawrence of Arabia." His mammoth book "The Seven Pillars of Wisdom" told the story of his exploits and championed the Arab Nationalist cause. It was largely due to its publication that the Arab nations of today became known to the European public and emerged into the twentieth century.

Sir John Glubb was born in England in 1897. He joined the Royal Engineers in 1915 and planned a career as a military officer in the British Army. After World War One he served with the Royal Air Force Intelligence Corps in Iraq but resigned his commission in 1926 to take a post with the Iraqi Army, helping to train their troops. Transferring to the Transjordan administration, he achieved fame as the Chief of General Staff to the Arab Legion. Glubb took on the task of turning a force of desert nomads into an efficient and orderly fighting force which in itself brought Jordan out of the desert and made it a legitimate country with a respected monarchy. I remember as a boy seeing movie newsreels in London theaters of Glubb and his "Arab Legion". I also remember how angry the British were when King Hussein fired him. Up to that point he was like a proud peacock of British Aristocracy at the head of the most advanced, and best-trained army in the Middle East.

It could well be argued that these two British Officers were responsible for forming the modern Arab nations of today. T.E. Lawrence encouraged them to stand up against the European Empires, and Glubb showed them how to train a modern army.

Glubb was finally fired by King Hussein in 1956 because he never was an Arabphile and always loyal to the British Crown. While Hussein was himself educated at Eton, he felt it was time to come out from under the British control and become equal with his former masters.

In the Spring of 2001 the Oxford Times proof of Lawrence's book sold at Christies Auction House in New York for almost one million dollars.

Section Three

MODERN PRINCES GO FORTH TO WAR

CHAPTER 8

Desert Warlords become Princes.

In order to understand anything of the Maelstrom of Middle Eastern Politics today, one must make some examination of the history of those descended from Mohammed and the Desert Mafia he founded. I shall attempt to do this as briefly as possible and perhaps with a little humor to humidify the dry desert atmosphere of the history.

As we have already discovered, Mohammed had several wives and many children. Since we know that it was the practice of his raiding parties to rape the women while attacking villages and caravans, many more women must presumably have carried his children. From this we can assume that his descendants today are numerous, to say the least. In any event all of the tribes and villages in Arabia eventually bowed to Mohammed's doctrine whether they were his children or not. There was no choice.

After the advent of Islam, Mohammed's followers and their descendants continued to carry out ruthless raids upon local tribes, caravans, and neighboring countries. It was not long before they had conquered the "fertile crescent" which stretched from Turkey in the north to Egypt in the south, while the center of the Islamic world continued to be Mecca, in Arabia. During the next few centuries the Moslem hordes swept through North Africa and across the Mediterranean to Spain and southern France. They took Italy and moved up from Turkey through the Balkans into Austria, Southern Russia, and in the east to India, Pakistan, and Afghanistan.

The Crusaders (1095 – 1274), who also plundered, murdered and raped, but officially did not have more than one wife, did little to release the Islamic stranglehold on the Middle East and North Africa. They built imposing castles, many of which remain today, maintained armies for a while, and finally left. They left behind not only their castles but also a few thousand red haired or blond, blue eyed, half Arab children whose descendants are still there today. There were many inter-Islamic battles as warlords took on each other's armies and small Islamic Empires warred against each other. There were wins and losses but only between Islamic armies. The Mongols came and went but nothing much changed until the Ottoman Turkish Empire began to grow in the 14th century and expand its territory. It continued to expand, particularly starting in the mid 15th century, when the Turks captured Constantinople and annexed Serbia, Bosnia, Herzegovina, and Albania all in the space of nine years. In 1473 they had become bold enough to make war on Persia and win, and two years later they took Venice which made the Turkish navy the master of the Aegean. In the first half of the 16th century the Turks conquered Egypt, part of Hungary and Austria, and seemed about to take over Europe. Turkey soon became the master of the Islamic world—taking Mecca, losing it, and capturing it again. In the mid 19th century Egypt experienced a renaissance of sorts and for a time beat back Turkey and captured Arabia and all the way up to Syria, only to lose most of it again to the Turks.

And so, as the twentieth century dawned, Turkey controlled most of the Islamic Empire while Britain and France occupied the North African Islamic states of Egypt and Morocco. Arab nationalist groups began to form with the aim of kicking the Turks out of what they considered to be Arab lands. In truth the only really Arab lands were the two empires of Arabia, the Najd and the Hejaz. The people of Syria were not Arabs but Syrians. The Iraqis were also not Arabs and the Lebanese were Phoenicians. The people of Israel were Jews with some people of mixed race who sometimes called themselves Palestinians. But, as usual the Arabs wanted it all.

The decisive events that would shape the next one hundred years or more began in 1914 when the Turks backed the Germans against the allies in the First World War. Up to now the story has been relatively simple with a variety of Arabs and Turks and other odd assortments like Egyptians, Afghans, and Burbers all fighting each other for small pieces of Mohammed's Empire. Now it will become decidedly more complicated as we shall see.

It has taken close to a century to discover exactly what World War One was all about. It was gloriously billed at the time as "The War to end all Wars." But it seems to have fallen a little bit short of that. Each of the countries purported to have noble aims, but it was mainly about breaking the tenth commandment, "Thou shalt not covet." Germany wanted to become a "world power" with colonies. The only way the Kaiser could think of to bring this about was to invade the African colonies of France and Belgium. If these colonies were added to the small amount of Africa that Germany already had, they would form a nice big block of territory to call "The German Empire." In Europe Germany wanted to control France, Belgium, Poland, the Ukraine, Latvia, and the Balkans, an area they called MittleEurope (Middle Europe). The African colonies would thus be called Mittle Africa. Part of this plan was to enlist the aid of the Turks as allies and then allow them to administer much of the colonies under German supervision. Of course Germany never had any intention of fulfilling these Turkish aspirations, but it had to outbid the Allies.

The Allies were no less prone to breaking the tenth commandment. France wanted the area of Alsace and Lorraine, the land between Germany and France. It also hoped that at the end of the war they would have advanced far enough into Germany to own the German coal mines in the Saar and Rhine which it would need in order to make full use of the iron ore in Alsace-Lorraine. Britain wanted to have naval supremacy around the world. Russia wanted Constantinople (Istanbul) because it controlled her access to the Mediterranean via the Black Sea. The only other ports Russia had were in the frozen north of her country which were iced over more than half the year, and the Black Sea offered year round navigation for the military and trade. The allies also persuaded Italy to join them by offering them part of the Turkish Empire at war's end.

Turkey joined the war in October 1914 believing that the Germans would win and that her faithful ally the Kaiser would share the spoils by allowing Turkey to administer half of Africa, all of the Middle East, and parts of Eastern Europe. The Turks were reasonably content that the Muslims in their Empire would lie low for the duration of the war, but they were wrong. The British in their usual skullduggerous manner went in the back door and convinced the Arabs (the real Arabs in Arabia) in the person of Hussein, descendant of the Prophet, Sharif of Mecca and Guardian of the Holy Places of Islam, to come in on their side against Turkey.

For a thousand years the head of the Beni Hashem family, direct descendants of the Prophet, had been Sharif of Mecca. The family, known in English as the Hashemites, was descended from the Prophet through his daughter Fatima and her husband Ali. The duplicitous Brits convinced Hussein that for his support in the war they would give him control over a confederation of three states, Hejaz (Arabia), Syria, and Iraq. All Hussein had to do was to make sure the Islamists in the region revolted against their Turkish occupiers.

At the beginning of World War One, you will remember, the Turks were in control of most of the Middle East including what they called Palestine. Britain promised the Palestinian Arabs independence from Turkey if the Islamists would rise up together against the Ottoman Empire and side with the Allies. These terms were spelled out in a series of letters known today as the "Husayn-McMahon correspondence."

The British were masters in the art of literary deception. If the government wanted to put forward a promise to another country which could later be reneged upon it appointed a semi-official go-between. This was usually a person of title, or a knight of the realm which gave their word all the strength of a true "gentleman's agreement" but at the same time was totally worthless. When the aggrieved party later came to the British government, it could simply say that the person had represented his own feelings and not those of the government. In the next few paragraphs we shall see three such instances.

The Husayn (Hussein) – McMahon correspondence took place in letters written between July 1915 and March 1916 between Sir Henry McMahon, British High Commissioner in Egypt, and Sharif Hussein ibn Ali in Mecca. McMahon's assurances of prizes galore caused Hussein, Sharif of Mecca to declare the independent state of Hejaz on June 5th 1916 with himself as its King. Declaring his state an ally of Great Britain, his two sons Faisal and Abdullah (King Hussein of Jordan's grandfather) led two Arab armies to conquer the lands of the north. The two lads marched their armies triumphantly towards the two countries their British allies had promised them, Syria and Iraq.

Meanwhile in the merry month of May, the Brits were at it again. Before the ink was properly dry on McMahon's final letter to Hussein, and before the old boy had a chance to announce his new Kingdom to the world, they had concluded agreements with the French and the Russians to divide up the same territory between them. This time they employed Sir Mark Sykes to write duplicitous letters to Georges Picot of France. Sykes was a British expert on the Orient, and Picot was a former French Consul in Beirut. In this "agreement" Sir Mark set forth the British government's proposal that France would have Lebanon, Syria and a few other areas. Britain would have Iraq plus the Israeli ports of Haifa and Akko (Acre). Russia would have Armenia and part of the Kurdish territory. Palestine would be international territory due to the many places of biblical interest. This agreement was made in secret with the French and Russians and ignored the agreement signed just two months earlier with the Sharif of Mecca. And this was not all – by any means.

Britain had also made a promise to the Jews that conflicted with both of the other promises. The circumstances of that declaration were as follows.

Britain badly needed three things that the Jews alone could provide. Chaim Weitzman the Russian Jewish Chemist now living in England had discovered new formulas for acetone and butyl alcohol, which were urgently needed for the war effort. Weizmann, an ardent Zionist who later became the first President of Israel, made the British backing of a country for the Jews in their ancestral homeland of Israel a condition for handing over the formula. The other urgent needs were for the support of American Jews to convince the United States to enter the war on the side of the Allies and for Russian Jews to push their government to stay in the battle alongside Britain.

This letter was written by British Foreign Minister Arthur James Balfour in agreement with British Jewish leaders and the cabinet and was sent to the 2nd Baron Rothschild on November 2, 1917:

Foreign Office
November 2nd, 1917

Dear Lord Rothschild,
I have much pleasure in conveying to you, on behalf of His Majesty's Government, the following declaration of sympathy with Jewish Zionist aspirations which has been submitted to, and approved by, the Cabinet.

"His Majesty's Government view with favour the establishment in Palestine of a national home for the Jewish people, and will use their best endeavours to facilitate the achievement of this object, it being clearly understood that nothing shall be done which may prejudice the civil and religious rights of existing non-Jewish communities in Palestine, or the rights and political status enjoyed by Jews in any other country."

I should be grateful if you would bring this declaration to the knowledge of the Zionist Federation.

Yours sincerely,
Arthur James Balfour

The final paragraph asking Lord Rothschild to bring the letter to the attention of the Zionist Federation was coded to mean that the British government was agreeing to their terms (the foundation of a Jewish State) in exchange for the favors requested from them. This declaration was formally approved by representatives of the allied governments at the Versailles Peace Conference in 1919 and was the basis of the League of Nations mandate for Palestine.

Once they had the formulas and the Americans entered the war, the wily English thought everyone would forget that promise. In fact they expected everyone to forget all the promises they had made.

The total and global dishonesty of the British was the seed of all the trouble that now exists in the Middle East. Coupled with Arab greed and fanatic Islamic violence, it has come back to haunt every one of the participants and leave the Israelis in a state of constant siege in their ancestral homeland.

While the politicians back in Europe were settling who would get what after the war, Lord Allenby, the British General, had moved his troops up from Cairo and taken Jerusalem from the Turks in December 1917.

Meanwhile, we must return to the desert with the two Hussein boys and their army. Prince Abdullah was lying low, trying not to be noticed while his brother Faisal managed the army with the help of T.E. Lawrence (Lawrence of Arabia). Eventually they arrived in Syria and joined Lord Allenby in surrounding Damascus and eventually conquering the city on October 3, 1918. The combined armies then spread out and mopped up the remainder of the Turkish resistance in the area and ended Ottoman rule in the Middle East.

The war ended and it was now time for the Brits to settle up and pay their debts to those who had helped. The only problem was that the British had made too many promises and had never had any intention of keeping any of them. There is an English proverb "All's fair in love and war," and they believe in it. The British tried to look the other way and pretend that they knew nothing of what was going on. But looking the other way and trying to manipulate the affairs of the Middle East at the same time has its pitfalls. Meanwhile the Bolsheviks decided to get in on the act.

While all of this "diplomacy" and warfare had been going on Lenin, Marx, Engels and Trotsky and their playmates had staged a revolution in Russia and plundered the Tzar's safe. In it they found copies of those British proposals to divide up the Middle East between Britain, France and Russia. They immediately let the whole world know how conniving and false the Bourgeois, Imperialist, Capitalist, Bankers and downtreaders of the masses were, and what they had done. Again the British tried to pretend that nothing had happened and kept doing business as usual.

The British had set up their own administration in Jerusalem and effectively ruled the rest of the country. But they would now have to convince the rest of the world that they had a right to be there. The Jews and the Palestinian Arabs each were waving pieces of paper showing that they were the legal recipients of the British promise of statehood, a promise that Britain had no right to make in the first place, and certainly not to both parties.

In February 1919 the Jerusalem Arabs held a conference with the Christians of the city in which they rejected the Balfour Declaration and proclaimed a Muslim State. On March 20th 1920 the Arabs held a conference in Damascus in which they predictably agreed with former rejection of the Balfour Declaration and elected Prince Faisal of Mecca King of Syria and "Palestine."

Further complicating matters, the allies held a conference of their own in July 1920 in San Remo, Italy, to formally divide up the former Ottoman Empire. They awarded Syria and Lebanon to France and Palestine to Britain. Russia of course got nothing because the legitimate government with whom the Sykes–Picot agreement had been made had been taken over by the Bolsheviks who were not considered nice people.

Now the French came knocking on King Faisal's door. Remember that he had been given British permission to form a Kingdom of Syria, which he ruled from Damascus. But since the British had also promised Syria to France in the Sykes-Picot agreement, the French wanted their prize. Since they had more guns than Faisal they forced him to give up his throne in July 1920 after just four months. This of course meant that he was also out of power in Jerusalem because the British wanted that for themselves.

In the same month, July 1920, the British Military administration in Jerusalem was replaced with a civilian one. The first British High Commissioner was announced as Sir Herbert Samuel, a Zionist Jew. This of course was designed to placate the Jews over the British failing to fully honor the Balfour Declaration, but did nothing to cool the anger of the Arabs who had already rioted in the Jewish quarter killing five Jews and wounding over 200. In addition the British authorities did allow a small concession to the Zionists by allowing 16,500 Jews to make Aliya (emigrate to Israel). In 1922 Britain announced that she did not contemplate that Palestine, as a whole should be a Jewish State, but that a Jewish National Home should be founded within Palestine.

Meanwhile back in Arabia, you will remember that there were two states. The pro-British one was the Hejaz under the Sharif of Mecca, Hussein ibn Ali. The other was the Nejd ruled by Sheik Al Saud who would later be the founder of Saudi Arabia. In 1923, Sharif Hussein lost control of Mecca to the Wahabees, a fundamentalist sect of Islam under the leadership of Sheik Al Saud

After Faisal was kicked out of Syria by the French, he was in danger of becoming another wanderer in the vast desert. But the British for once seeming to have a conscience told him he could now be King of Iraq in August 1921 and his family reigned there till 1958.

Abdullah, the other son of Sharif Hussein, was proclaimed Amir of Transjordan, a new country that the British formed out of their mandate from the League of Nations, the Southern part of Greater Syria.

This brings us to relatively modern times and we will be in a far better position to understand what happened later in the various new states and Kingdoms. One amusing side note remains however.

During the Gulf War Saddam Hussein of Iraq sneeringly addressed King Hussein of Jordan as "Sharif," reminding him that it was the Saudis who had stolen his birthright as Sharif of Mecca. He then called the King of Saudi Arabia not " Sharif of Mecca and Guardian of the Holy Places" but "King of the Nejd," the small and poor Arab kingdom from which his family sprang.

So the fourteen hundred-year-old feud among Mohammed's followers continues to this day.

BBC interview December 15, 2001 withLeon Wieseltier, Literary Editor of "New Republic."

BBC Why do you think the Bush Administration waited so long to release a video (The Bin Laden tape) they say they found in Afghanistan a month ago?

LW I think that *the U.S. Government is trying to calibrate a policy that would be exquisitely sensitive to the Arab World* for a whole variety of good and bad reasons. That's what slowed down its release.

BBC But do you believe there's any prospect that this release will turn the tide of public opinion, which I know from my own recent visits to the Middle East, is extremely hostile to the United States?

LW No. No I think that the irony of this is that it will have almost no impact at all upon people who do not wish to believe in Bin Laden's responsibility for the attack.

BBC I think one of the key points of this interview is the presence of this Saudi Gentleman and the interest that Bin Laden appears to have in the reaction to September 11th. Does that tell us anything unsettling about Saudi Arabia?

LW Look there's much unsettling about Saudi Arabia and by my lights *the great scandal in American Foreign Policy at this point is the refusal of the American Government to face up to the nature of the Saudi* *regime* and to the character of its relations with the Saudi regime. I mean sure, sure, this video belongs not just in the Bin Laden File, it belongs in the Saudi file.

BBC So what should the administration be doing differently?

LW *The United States gets about 17% of its oil from Saudi Arabia. That's not nothing, but it's far from everything. The administration* in 1991, and again now *has allowed the Saudi government's view of its own interests essentially to dominate American policy in the region.* I think that the administration is exploiting the fact that *the American population is not prepared to accept any serious energy policy.*

BBC Do you think then that the war against terrorism should be take not to Iraq or Somalia as has been suggested but towards Saudi Arabia?

LW I think that *a very grim and determined reassessment of the American policy toward Saudi Arabia is the greatest single priority right now.* The United States is fighting a war against terrorism in central Asia but *this is not a central Asian problem. It's an Arab problem* that found a refuge in Central Asia. *There's not a single figure that I've heard of in the High Command of Al-Quaida who is not an Egyptian, a Saudi, or a Yemeni.*

BBC And that was Leon Wieseltier, Literary Editor of "New Republic."

In a nutshell the above interview shows Mr. Wieseltier's view that our Government in this and the last administrations has been lopsided in that it has bowed to the will of the Saudis rather than what is good for the American people. A very grim and determined reassessment of our policy towards Saudi Arabia is the greatest single priority right now because it is they who control the whole terror scenario. "It is an Arab problem."

This book will show why it is "an Arab problem." The false religion of Islam started with Arabs (Saudi Arabia) and it continued to be dictated by Saudis. Yet our government has long bowed and kowtowed to these monsters. It is time to break free of their grip, because it will soon be too late.

CHAPTER 9

Princes on a Sandpile

During World War One the British supported Husein ibn Ali the Sheikh of the Hejaz, one of the two rival states in the land of Arabia. Their support gave him the confidence to proclaim himself king of all the Arabs, which meant the two states of Hejaz and Najd. This so infuriated Ibn Saud Abdul Aziz sheik of Najd that he invaded the neighboring state in 1919 and with the help of the Wahabees, a fundamentalist sect of Islam, he undermined Hussein's leadership from within. Hussein abdicated in favor of his son Ali who was then deposed in 1925. In 1926 ibn Saud declared himself King of Hejzaz and Najd and all its Dependencies (in other words King of all the Arabs). On September 18, 1932, ibn Saud changed the name of the combined Kingdom to Saudi Arabia.

During the first few years there were disputes with Yemen and Egypt, and the borders of the country were changed frequently. Traditionally borders in the desert were based on the location of the various tribes under the control of a warlord. Since Bedouin tribes move constantly, the borders simply could not be put on a map. Eventually borders with Kuwait, Jordan, and Iraq were set by international agreement in 1930, but the borders with the Gulf States were left unmarked until much later.

Oil was discovered along the Persian Gulf in the 1930s but was not exploited until 1944 when Aramco (the Arabian American Oil Company) began production in earnest. Until then the Saudis' only revenue sources were from the annual Pilgrimage to Mecca and support from the United States and Britain. The Saudis finally began to realize the wealth that was under their sand when in 1949 they discovered that Aramco was paying more taxes to the United States Government than they were paying in revenues to Saudi Arabia. In 1950 the Saudi Princes demanded that they be paid 50% of the profits of the company.

Following the death of the founder of the country, ibn Saud, in 1953 Saudi Arabia went through some difficult times in determining the future course of the country. The late king had despised the changes that were threatening to turn his kingdom into an almost western nation. Roads and cities had been built in a very short space of time, and one of his sons was in the habit of frequent and costly foreign travel. The new King Saud, who felt much as his father had, and his brother Faysal, the jet-setter, were frequently at odds about the fast moving changes. A civil war in the old tribal fashion broke out with Faysal becoming the new King. Since then the kingdom has been administered by the royal family with several of them having the position of King, Prime Minister, Oil Minister, etc. in turn.

The present King, Fahd, was born in Riyadh in 1921 as son of King ibn Saud. He held a variety of posts in the government including those of minister of education, interior minister, and deputy Prime Minister, before becoming King upon the death of Khalid. He has had a stroke and is not likely to live much longer. Meanwhile Islamic fundamentalists threaten the Saudi throne and could stage a civil war at almost any time. At one point religious extremists took over the Al-Harram mosque in Mecca for two weeks before being captured and killed. Incidents of rioting by Shi'ite Muslims are taking place in several locations.

In 1960 the Saudis were leaders in the establishment of OPEC (Organization of Petroleum Exporting Countries), with a Saudi Prince as chairman, which gave them the threat of power over the western nations who were so dependent on their oil. They were also founders of the Arab League, which tries to bring the various Islamic Arab nations into a consensus on many political issues. However there are problems even with the Arab League. First of all the only true Arabs in the group are the Saudis themselves, and secondly, no two Arabs ever seem able to completely agree with one another on any issue. Jews will quickly agree that this is a trait common to both sides of the family and have a saying "wherever there are two Jews you will find at least three opinions."

The Saudis organized a boycott against the United States in 1973 when we backed Israel during the Arab-Israeli war. These people have no love for the United States or for Europe. They tolerate us because we are good for business and because they know we will help them in time of war as we did in 1990 when Iraq attacked Kuwait. At that time the

United States sent in 230,000 troops to defend Saudi Arabia and supplied the best and latest equipment. The Saudis are quick to change sides, shown by the fact that during the Gulf War they ejected all of the Yemeni and Jordanian citizens who were working there and replaced them with Kuwaitis and the Americans who just before that had been called "*The Great Satan*." The Saudis have since established ties with China, Russia, and their former enemy Iran. The Chinese have supplied them with sophisticated rockets capable of reaching any part of the Middle East with nuclear, chemical, and biological warheads. The Saudis are fanatically opposed to Israel and will certainly turn against the United States and shut off our petroleum supplies on a whim. This is why our government treats them with so much care and bows to their Islamic whims. For instance American servicemen during the Gulf War were not permitted to wear crosses or Stars of David for fear of upsetting those they were defending.

The question is how far will the Saudis go in pressuring the United States to fall into line with Islamic demands? And more important than that, how far will the United States go in obeying their orders? We have already gone too far.

Crown Prince Abdullah of Saudi Arabia told Washington ten days before the Islamic Atrocities of September 11 that US policy towards the Arab-Israeli conflict had become untenable. Who are these sons of desert bandits to dictate our policy? Yet it was only a matter of days before President Bush announced that he would be backing a Palestinian state.

Sources in Riyadh said the secret letter sent by Abdullah to George Bush was part of a dialogue started in Paris in June between Crown Prince Abdullah and Colin Powell. So the Bush statement was not made, as we thought, to encourage Islamist States to join the coalition against terrorism. It was in the works long before September 11, and was our subservient answer to the Saudi threat.

The Saudi letters said the US stance on Israel was making it impossible for the Saudi leadership to follow policies that were in our interests and theirs.

Mr Bush is said to have written back to assure the Saudis that he clearly understood the message.

In a statement following Mr. Bush's capitulation on the issue of a "Palestinian State," the Crown Prince is reported to have praised Mr. Bush, saying the kingdom appreciated the move. In other words George is a good boy. Does this mean that the United States is now permanently on a leash held by the rulers of a sand pile? I believe it does unless something is done to reaffirm America's leadership in the world.

Saudi Arabia has backed the US campaign against Bin Laden but will not allow us to extend it to other Islamic countries. Sheikh Saleh bin Mohammad al-Lahidan, head of the country's higher judicial council, countered Osama bin Laden's calls for a general Islamic uprising by stressing that *jihad* should be fought for the good of the Muslim nation, not its destruction.

This in itself is a very interesting statement. He is saying that the *jihad* can be used under limited circumstances against an Islamist group, for instance if the group is in disfavor with the Saudi Royal Family, but otherwise only against the Infidels. This is in sharp contrast to the statements by some Islamists recently that *Jihad* does not mean Holy War, but rather a spiritual or philosophical war. It is also interesting to note that he speaks of the Islamic Nation as an entity, not Islamic Nations. In other words, Islamists are all one when it comes to opposing, for instance, the *Great Satan*, as they call the United States.

Saudi Princess Takes on "The Great Satan"

The December 19th issue of the Orlando Sentinel offers an account of the activities of her Royal Highness Buniah al-Saud (aka "Bonnie" to her few American friends). Her majesty arose for a breakfast of grits and creamed wheat along with many other guests in the Orange County Jail at 4am.

Bonnie's royal gown was exchanged Monday night for an orange jumpsuit after she was booked on charges of felony battery against her Indonesian maid. Her Royal Highness is said to have beaten up the poor girl and pushed her down seventeen stairs. Then for an encore she is accused of stealing her former driver's big screen TV and furniture and selling it for $6,000 to a neighbor. Well, what's a princess to do in America? Good help is almost impossible to find and if they mess up, they should be ready to suffer for it.

The Princess left town in a huff Tuesday night for Washington DC where they know how to treat royalty. She was bonded out at $5,000 and must return to the Magic Kingdom for the criminal trial. Meanwhile her Orlando attorney is holding her passport to prevent her escape back to the sandpile. Do they really think she can't get another passport and hop aboard a Saudi aircraft within hours? But then she obviously likes it here, and a few million dollars will probably buy some mighty fine attornying.

We hear that the "royal one" has been studying English on the grounds of the University of Central Florida and may graduate on December 21st.

The accusations were no surprise to the State Department. They report that Saudis frequently beat up their servants. Local Police didn't know this was a common thing and they attempted to arrest her. She protested that she had "diplomatic immunity," which was backed up by the Saudi Embassy. It was discovered later that this was a lie and the arrest took place anyway. The United States is known to Islamists as "The Great Satan."

So! What else is new? Nice try princess!

CHAPTER 10

The Hashemites Of Jordan

The present ruler of Jordan is King Abdullah II who ascended the throne on February 7, 1999, immediately after the death of his father King Hussein. Jordan is considered one of the most progressive of the Middle Eastern Arab Kingdoms and maintains a friendly relationship with the United States and with Israel. However it must be remembered that Jordan took the side of Saddam Hussein during the Gulf War. The reason for that will become obvious as we take a brief look into its history.

The country of Trans-Jordan, formerly part of the Turkish Ottoman Empire, was founded in 1921 as a British protectorate. The British then divided it into two pieces in 1922, forming the states of Palestine on the west bank of the Jordan River and Trans-Jordan (across Jordan) on the east bank. As usual the Brits ignored the rights of the people who lived in the area and simply rewarded those who had helped them in the war.

The British Government had promised Sharif Hussein of Mecca that he would have Syria, Iraq, and "Palestine" as his prize for helping the British Army defeat the Ottoman Empire, which had been allied with Germany in the First World War.

The Hashemite family claims to be descended directly from the "prophet" Mohammed through his daughter Fatima and her husband Ali bin Abi Talib, who was also first cousin to the "prophet." They were desert dwellers and shepherds until they won the title of Sharif of Mecca, a title held by the head of the family from 1201 to 1925.

During the Great Arab Revolt against Ottoman rule in 1916, Al-Hussein bin Ali, Sharif of Mecca and King of the Arabs, sided with the British and sent his two sons Abdullah and Faisal off to liberate the lands in the north. Having helped the British army to take Jordan, Lebanon, Syria, Iraq, Palestine, and Hijaz (part of Arabia), Faisal was given the Kingdom of Syria and Abdullah got Jordan. Faisal was kicked out of Syria by the French and was then given Iraq as a consolation prize. The truth is that there wasn't much to write home about in Syria, Iraq, or Jordan. They were little more than vast desert wastelands with a few villages and Bedouin camps.

King Abdullah

King Abdullah reigned for thirty years and, with the help of Britain, formed a Democratic Government, built a fairly nice capital, and established himself as the first monarch of what has turned out to be an imposing line. Jordan was granted independence from Britain in 1946. Abdullah declared war on Israel as soon as the State of Israel was announced, and the Arab Legion, which had been trained by Glubb Pasha together with six other Islamic Armies, did fairly well against the unarmed Jews. To their credit the Jordanians were able to hold on to East Jerusalem and the West Bank of the Jordan river and this turned out to be a bad omen for the King. If they had lost Jerusalem Abdullah might not have died as he did. It had been his habit to drive to Jerusalem for Friday prayers at the Mosque of Al Aksa, one of the two mosques built on top of the Temple of God on Temple Mount. On July 20, 1951, Abdullah was assassinated in the mosque by a Palestinian Terrorist. The future King Hussein was with his grandfather and was only saved from the bullet that hit him, by a medal recently given to him by the King. It should probably be explained that the Palestinians in those days were demanding that the Jordanian occupation be ended, much as today they are demanding the same of Israel.

King Talal

Abdullah's son Talal ascended the Hashemite throne but was replaced with his son Hussein just a year later due to Talal's mental illness.

King Hussein

Educated at Eton College and Sandhurst Military Academy in England, King Hussein was a model of charm, diplomacy, good looks, and wise leadership. From the beginning of his reign he faced serious problems with the Palestinians who form the majority of his subjects. The Hashemites were Arabs from Arabia and therefore foreigners in the land. Hussein survived a Palestinian attempted coup, which very nearly succeeded and executed up to 40,000 Palestinians to teach them a lesson. He made peace with Israel in 1994 and made a very special trip to Israel after the killing of several Israeli schoolchildren at a border park. He came to the homes of their parents and knelt before them, asking his personal forgiveness for the crazed act of one of his citizens. Upon the assassination of Yitzak Rabin, King Hussein, a first class pilot, passed an El Al aircraft and radioed his condolences to the Captain of the Israel plane, and to the Israeli people. If other Islamic leaders had one percent of the wisdom of this man, there would be no trouble in the Middle East. Although a Muslim, Hussein could not be described as a fanatic when dealing with non-Muslims. However the slaughter of 20,000 of his Palestinian subjects might be considered a little excessive.

King Abdullah II

The present King of Jordan, King Abdullah took over as king on February 7, 1999, the day after his father's death from cancer. He is still a somewhat unknown quantity although it is hoped he will follow in his father's footsteps. He is certainly not without education and intelligence. He first attended Islamic schools in Amman, with secondary education at St. Edmund's school in England and Eaglebrook School and Deerfield Military Academy in the United States. He then went to the Royal Military Academy at Sandhurst and a year at Oxford.

Back in Jordan Abdullah entered his own country's military and worked his way up to the rank of Captain. He was an instructor in the Air Force Helicopter Anti-Tank wing and qualified as a Cobra Attack Helicopter Pilot. He later saw service in several other areas of his country's armed forces with a final rank of Major General. He is a qualified Frogman, pilot, free-fall parachutist, and former Jordanian National Racing Champion. Don't be surprised if he represents Jordan in the Olympic Games.

Surely no Arab Prince is more qualified to lead a country than Abdullah. He appears to have the wisdom and intelligence of his father, but we will have to wait and see where his allegiances lie. His wife is Palestinian. This is not necessarily a bad thing. I know many wonderful Palestinians. But, it is just possible that he might be persuaded to take the Palestinian view against Israel.

Politics the most sleazy of professions.

BBC NEWS announced January 1st 2001 that the British Government had been asked on September 21, 1970 to relay a message from King Hussein of Jordan to Israeli Prime Minister Golda Meir asking Israel to bomb Syrian forces who were backing the Palestinian insurrection against his throne. The announcement of this incredible story was suppressed under a British law until 30 years after the event.

Then British prime Minster Edward Heath "passed the buck" on to Washington because he was afraid the Palestinians might win and that they would then turn against Britain for suggesting an Israeli intervention. So, instead of helping, or even asking the Israelis to help their old friend and ally King Hussein, the typically selfish Brits decided to pass the message to the Americans and let them take the consequences. Golda Meir happened to be in New York at the time and the U.S. government sent the message to her. It is not clear yet what her reaction might have been but the Israelis used constraint and limited their help to supplying arms and espionage information to the King.

One can only imagine what might have happened had Israel gone to the King's rescue and helped him wipe out a few million Palestinians. The Islamist States were not strong enough to retaliate. Syria would have been totally beaten and Jordan would have been very much beholden to Israel. The expansion of Islam and its accompanying worldwide violence would have been seriously slowed and perhaps even stopped. But Israel was undoubtedly afraid of being caught in the middle by the fickle politics of both the United States and Britain. Jews would have been the scapegoats once again.

CHAPTER 11

Prince Saddam the Insane

If you were able to travel to Iraq today you would see many sights of biblical importance. But, without a doubt, the most exciting discovery would be one about sixty miles from Baghdad on the shores of the Euphrates River. Here you would find the rebuilt city of Babylon. That's right—Babylon!

The city has been rebuilt with painstaking accuracy, and you could walk through the great gates of the ancient city and down the Street of Processions to the Palace. Here you could enter the banqueting hall of King Nebuchadnezzer where Daniel saw the writing on the wall 2600 years ago. You might descend the stone steps to the banks of the Euphrates where the Hanging Gardens, one of the seven wonders of the ancient world, were located. You could see all of this if Iraq were a free country and not controlled by one of the most dangerous lunatics in the world. All of this rebuilding has been made possible by the wonderful generosity of Saddam Insane the Iraqi President. While Iraqi children were dying of hunger, Saddam spent multiplied millions on renovating a historical sight.

Saddam Hussein did not spend a fortune on this project just for educational or archeological reasons. He believes that he is the reincarnation of King Nebuchadnezzer, destined by Allah to restore the glory of Babylon and to lead the Arab Nation in the last great *Jihad* that will finally overthrow the *infidels* and put the whole world under the control of Islam. He wants to rule his Empire from Nebuchadnezzer's palace.

Saddam was born in 1937 into a peasant family in a village near Tikrit. This small town on the banks of the Euphrates was also the birthplace of the great twelfth century Sultan and military leader *Saladin*. Saddam was orphaned at an early age and went to live on a melon farm with an uncle who was a devout Muslim. He entered primary school at age nine and later studied in a Baghdad secondary school.

Joining the Arab Baath socialist party in 1956, he took part in a coup attempt against King Faisal. Faisal was one of the two brothers—Faisal and Abdullah—sons of the Sharif who came from Mecca to claim their inheritance from the British. Abdullah received the country of Jordan. Faisal was given Syria, but was kicked out of there and finally got Iraq as a booby prize. When this attempt failed, a rival group to the Baath Party headed by Abdul Karim Kassem killed the king. Saddam Hussein was chosen, along with nine other young men, to plan the killing of Kassem. (What a merry life these Muslims lead! If they're not killing innocent people in Jerusalem and New York, they kill each other.) The attempt failed but left Hussein wounded and a wanted man. He escaped across the desert on a donkey and, unfortunately for the whole world, he lived to fight another day.

Gamal Abdul Nasser, the Egyptian revolutionary leader, heard about the exploits of young Saddam and invited him to come to Cairo to attend Cairo University Law School. Gamal Abdul knew a bright young student when he saw one and felt that anyone who would attempt to assassinate Kassem should be a lawyer. Saddam studied at the University until someone else was able to complete the job he had failed to do in Baghdad. In 1963, following the assassination of Kassem, he returned home and continued his law studies in Baghdad while he worked his way up to the leadership of the Baath Party. But Saddam soon decided that he had studied enough and it was time to take a short cut on the way to his law degree. At the time appointed for his examination, he appeared at the University armed and with four bodyguards. The University President was able to see that Saddam deserved the degree and handed it over immediately.

From the University Saddam decided to use his degree to go immediately to work. It was a critical time of his life. He was head of the Baath Party, had a law degree to prove his ability to govern the country, and couldn't see any reason not to – just do it. He made an announcement to the press and took over the Presidential Palace, calling himself "Mr. President." He has never looked back.

In 1972 Hussein began the nationalization of the petroleum industry by seizing the property of American, British, Dutch, and French companies to fund his transformation of Iraq. The truth is that he has done wonderful things with the profits from Iraqi oil—including water purification, bringing electricity to almost every home in the country, building highways, housing, and hospitals. A massive compulsory education program was started in 1978 with higher education aimed at the creation of a "new technological Arab generation."

Hussein became the subject of a carefully orchestrated publicity campaign of monumental proportions. Giant portraits of him appeared everywhere, and he appeared on TV almost every night helping farmers with their harvest, visiting hospitals or giving candy to children, all with a background of soft music. His virtues were extolled in popular songs, poems, stories and movies. He even had a telephone line installed for citizens to call him and talk about their problems. Meanwhile most western new media were banned. Also, no one was allowed to own a typewriter without a special license.

Hussein has been married to his first cousin, a primary school teacher, since 1963. He reads history and political theory and owns a luxury yacht and over two hundred business suits, military uniforms, and tribal costumes. The inconsistency between his benign image and his brutally repressive rule can be explained according to the "Wall Street Journal" of June 13th 1980 as his "Jekyll and Hyde personality." Saddam Hussein is responsible for the poison gassing of hundreds of thousands of his own people, for purges of his own military leaders and advisors, and even the murder of many members of his own family.

Iraq has nuclear weapons as well as a vast array of chemical and biological weapons capable of carrying their payloads to all parts of the Middle East and Europe. American and Soviet aircraft, tanks, and artillery have been augmented by Chinese weapons of mass destruction and other weapons produced in Iraqi laboratories and factories. Since the International Weapons Inspectors were forced to leave the country, plants have gone once again into full production with the help of Chinese, Russian, and North Korean specialists and scientists.

The Islamic religion has been the gateway to power for this fanatical, genocidal, insane dictator. He hates Israel and the United States. He hates all Jews and all Christians. He truly believes that he is the reincarnation of Nebuchadnezzer, king of Babylon.

Now Saddam is thumbing his nose at the whole civilized world. We know that he has a great number of weapons of mass destruction including nuclear warheads, scud missiles, poison gas, and weapons capable of spreading bacteria over half the nations of the world. Yet our government has not the will power to stand up to him because they would have to override both France and Germany who want to do business with Iraq, and because we have big business interests in the United States who want to do business also as soon as the Europeans have paved the way. America would rather bully little Israel into giving away land to the Islamists.

Why has the United States government spent over two billion dollars of American taxpayers' money to arm Saddam Hussein? Probably for the same reason we armed all of the other countries who later turned against us. It's good for our arms business, and the arms dealers have plenty of lobbyists in Washington.

Looking over some of my newspaper and magazine clippings of the patriotic endeavors of Saddam Insane, I offer these for your further enlightenment.

Associated Press February 29, 1996.
Saddam Hussein purges rivals.
Targets own grandchildren.

The piece explains that Saddam's two sons-in-law together with their families and their supporters had been murdered by Saddam's two loyal sons, Odai and Qusai. The story, in case you have forgotten it, deals with

Lt..General Hussein Kamal al-Majid and his brother Col. Saddam Kamel who were married to Saddam's daughters Raghad and Rana. The girls had gone to live in Jordan with their husbands who just couldn't take any more of their father-in-law. When Saddam lured them back to Iraq with promises of forgiveness and better conditions, he first forced his daughters to divorce their husbands and then killed the rest of their families including 10-year-old Ali and 7-year-old Ahmed.

How is it possible that anyone could trust a religious system that promotes such hatred and terrorism? It must be clear that Hussein's two sons are just like their father, but which of them will kill the other to take over when the father dies?

U.S. News and World Report February 18, 1998
Moving Target.

This report shows how Saddam Hussein has built chemical weapons plants in Sudan and transferred nuclear material to Algeria. It was pieced together from Israeli, American, and German intelligence sources. Dozens of Iraqi scientists are reported to have moved to Libya where they have set up a biological weapons plant.

The transfers of these materials started even before the Gulf War when the Iraqis realized they would be bombed. These plants in a variety of Islamic countries, not just the three mentioned, are in full production still, churning out some of the most terrible weapons imaginable.

Among other things, Iraq moved 400 scud missiles plus an assortment of chemical weapons to Sudan. Then it smuggled 27.5 pounds of highly enriched uranium 235 to Jordan and on to Sudan. So, while King Hussein was smiling at us and having dinners at the White House, he was helping Saddam Hussein move materials capable of destroying many thousands, and possibly millions of Americans to safekeeping in Sudan. This is natural and normal. King Hussein was an Islamist. It is natural for all Islamists to help each other when it comes to destroying

America. While, as I have said, King Hussein was one of the best of the Arab Princes, he still hated us and so does his son. We must always be on our guard against all of them.

Saddam Hussein has already realized a large part of his aim to become a leader of the "Arab Nation." While we have been busy trying to detect war materials in Iraq itself, he has been shipping the stuff all over the Middle East. He now has strategic interests including weapons plants in Libya, Algeria, and Sudan. These are, even now, producing nuclear, biological, and chemical weapons for the madman. In addition he has facilities in Yemen and Afghanistan and probably several other countries. It will do little good to bomb Iraq when Saddam's weapons are in so many countries. We will have to take on all of them if we want to stop the madness.

London Daily Telegraph November 19, 2000
Saddam Stockpiling Deadly Chemical Weapons.

Ah! The Daily Telegraph! This was the newspaper I grew up with. Like the BBC, it could always be relied upon.

In this report Christina Lamb gives us information about the stockpiling of chemical weapons in schools and hospitals in Iraq. Satellite imaging has revealed Saddam's Republican guards moving vast quantities of these weapons including 610 tons of chemicals for the production of VX nerve gas, so deadly that one drop can kill a person. Imagine how many would be destroyed with 610 tons. He also has anthrax so potent that one teaspoon is enough to dissolve the kidneys, livers, and lungs of a million people. Think of one vacuum flask of this released in New York with the wind blowing in the right direction and you'll realize why it is so important for every American to understand the threat. We must demand that our government do more than apply cosmetics to the problem.

London Daily Telegraph January 29, 2001
Saddam has made two atomic bombs.

This report quotes an Iraqi defector as saying that Iraq has two fully operational nuclear bombs and is working to produce others. The defector, a military engineer who left Iraq just after the United Nations Arms Inspectors were forced out of the country, says, "Before the UN Inspectors came, there were 47 factories involved in the project. Now there are 64."

Reuters February 24th 2001
BND on Saddam Nukes.

Reuters News Service reveals that Iraq will be able to menace its neighbors with nuclear weapons within three years and fire a missile at Europe by 2005 according to the BND (German Intelligence Service). But other sources say he has that capability right now. Perhaps the BND is afraid of causing panic in Europe.

The BND goes on to say that Saddam has increased purchases abroad for the ingredients for his biological weapons.

London Daily Telegraph September 30. 2001
Saddam has Germ Warfare Arsenal.

Jessica Berry in Beirut filed this report in which she tells us that Saddam Hussein has ordered his top scientists to stop work on nuclear projects because they are too expensive, and concentrate on germ warfare and chemical weapons which are much cheaper and easier to deliver. Remember, he does already have two nuclear bombs.

Berry's sources include a top Iraqi nuclear physicist who recently defected. "Over the past six months 3,000 physicists have been working flat out on secret programs to develop both toxins and the means to deliver them to lethal effect."

This scientist formerly worked at the "Atomic Energy Organization" in Baghdad and had to get out because of his growing horror of the regime. "I was asked to examine hundreds of complicated and dangerous toxins," he said. "They were very easy to use to create germs. You could put them in water or steam, throw them in the air, or sow them in the soil. We developed nerve gas, botulism, and anthrax. All these substances were tested on Iraqi prisoners, mainly Kurds and Shi'ites in Radwania jail in west Baghdad." Western intelligence agents have confirmed the use of prisoners and that at least thirty of them died from the experiments. In other cases hundreds of Iraqi soldiers have died when exposed to the toxins.

Note that "The Butcher of Baghdad" experiments on his Islamist brothers, Kurds and Shi'ites. These are the people he loves who also worship Allah. Imagine what he will do to the infidels.

Among the vehicles for distributing these chemical and biological agents to the enemies of Allah, Saddam is producing rockets with the help of the Chinese and also pilotless "drone" aircraft which can fly under the radar and drop a payload as much as 700 miles away. Most of the parts are imported from companies in Thailand, the Philippines, and even Italy.

If our government caves in to Islamic pressure at home and abroad and does not destroy every weapon and factory in Iraq, the Iraqis will certainly attack us in the very near future with biological and chemical weapons. A simple vacuum flask taken to the top of the Empire State building could wipe out three or four million New Yorkers in a matter of a few hours. The World Trade Center bombing would be almost totally forgotten and worth only a short paragraph in history books.

But will our government act?

If we do not act NOW, what chance will we have of defending ourselves against these madmen four of five years from now? We know from recent events that they do not even care if they die in an attack. American Muslims will gladly give their lives because they believe they will gain immediate entrance into paradise.

I have offered here only snippets from one tenth of my files. Do I need to continue?

The sanctions imposed on Iraq at the end of the Gulf War were designed to prevent Saddam from continuing his reign of terror outside the country. But the Europeans began to capitulate almost immediately and the Islamic Governments were absolutely against them from the beginning. Why was this? The Europeans all have very large and vocal Islamic populations who threatened them with internal civil unrest. The Islamic Governments refused to condone enforcement by any government of an infidel nation. America still doesn't get it. The Muslims resent interference in the affairs of any Islamic country by anyone who is not Muslim. We will have to decide if we can or cannot live in a world of Muslim dominance in which Muslims dictate to us. If we want to have petroleum to fuel our cars and drive our trucks, we must act now while we still can. Islam is fast approaching the time of being able to dictate every move we make.

NOTE It has been brought to my attention that I mis-spelled Saddam's last name twice in this chapter. I must take this opportunity to apologize to him and at the same time assure him that the misspelling was entirely deliberate.

The Biggest Lie

Almost every day for the past year we have heard one major lie broadcast over and over again until we have been brainwashed. I am convinced that many people in the United States actually believe it because it has been drummed into our heads so many times like a mantra.

The Muslims and their fellow travelers, who control our Television and newspaper newsrooms have made sure that we hear it over and over again. It is the stupid Palestinian assertion that

"We are fighting for our lives against Israeli aggression."

The simple truth is that there is no Israeli aggression. The Israelis want peace and to be left alone in their own land. The Muslims constantly attack innocent, peaceful Israeli Citizens in their own country. There have been more than 8,000 terrorist attacks in the past year. Only a handful were attacks by frustrated Israelis against Palestinians. Almost all of them were by Islamic militants against peaceful Israelis.

The Israeli Army has been forced to retaliate against this mindless violence. For instance Islamists have kept up a constant bombardment of the Israeli suburb of Gilo from houses in the neighboring Palestinian Christian village of Beit Sahur. The Israelis have been forced to build a wall between the two to protect themselves, but still the Jihad fighters attack them. Israel has on several occasions sent tanks into Beit Sahur and demolished the houses from which the attackers were firing. This leaves the Christian Arab population without homes and Israel is blamed. But it is the Muslims who are to blame.

If the Islamists could be forced to stop attacking Israelis there would be immediate peace. Israel has been ready for peace since the first day. Yet we are told daily that the Israelis are the aggressors.

Chapter 12

Prince of Damascus

If you want to know the acorn, look to the Oak
                                                    Syrian proverb

When Bashar al Assad assumed the throne of his father in June of 2000 he was not quite sure what to do. In fact he could hardly believe that he was there at all. To all of Syria, and most of the world, it was as if a giant vacuum cleaner had suddenly scooped Hafez-al-Assad off the face of the earth and left a big open space into which everybody fell topsy-turvy, wondering which end was up. Who would succeed him as President? Surely not his son Bashar. He had no experience. But Basher's older brother Basil had died in a car crash, and his uncle Rifaat would serve his own agenda and not that of Hafez. Basher was the only one to carry on the family business.

With a majority of Syrians being of the Sunni Faith (of Islam) there was the ever present possibility of a coup against the Alawite, Assad Family who were in disarray. In spite of their command of top army posts, anything could happen. After all, the troops and many of the junior officers were Sunnis, and junior officers had revolted before in so many countries from Iraq and Syria to Libya and Egypt. So Crown Prince Assad was quickly sworn in to take his father's place, and the repressive regime of thirty years standing continued to grind its opposition into the dust.

Syria has a population of about fifteen million, of whom 86% are Muslims. The constitution adopted in 1973 calls for the law to be based on the Khoran although Assad frequently overrode the laws when dealing with anything he considered bordering on insurrection. While only 10% of the population—including the Assad family and the senior army officers—are Alawites, they maintain power by ruthlessly destroying anyone who rebels against them. They always know when trouble is brewing by using no fewer than fifteen different security organizations, each spying on everybody including each other. The birthrate in Syria is one of the highest in the world, and half of the population is under 25. There is little work, and income from their very small oil production does little to boost the economy. This is a country ready for revolution.

What kind of man is Bashar? How will he govern the country? His father's advisors and military commanders are still there, and they will guide Bashar in the ways of his father. But what should we really expect from the young President of Syria? Let us look for the answer to the oak tree from which the acorn sprang.

The late Syrian President Hafez al-Assad was born in 1928 or in 1930 (nobody is quite sure), in Quadra. He was the first from his small backward town to get any real education and left for secondary school in Latakia. He was soon involved in the movement to drive the French Colonials out of Syria, which was accomplished in 1946. At age 16 he joined the Arab Ba'ath Socialist party, similar to the one Saddam joined in neighboring Iraq. Minorities in Syria such as the Alawites were anxious for a movement to rid their country of the ruling class landowners and also the Sunni majority rule. Assad's education continued in Syrian Military colleges at a time when the governments were changing frequently due to coups and revolutions. The country depended more and more upon the Soviet Union for defense, agricultural assistance, and cash flow.

Hafez joined the Syrian Air Force and was sent to Moscow for further training. As a member of the Ba'ath party he was a believer in Soviet style Socialism and soon caught the eye of his superiors as a bright student and a loyal officer. He was promoted quickly and in 1963, when the Arab Ba'ath Party came to power, he was chosen as Commander of the Air Force. Three years later, after another coup (this time inside the Ba'ath), Assad was made Minister of Defense and kept this post until 1970 when he seized power and became President.

During the cold war he was one of the most important men the Soviets had in the Middle East. They were his benefactors for the first twenty years of his reign, supplying him with intelligence reports and also the latest weapons, aircraft, and tanks. Soviet Military advisors were seen in Damascus and on every Army and Air Force base in the country. In turn Assad was one of Moscow's most loyal supporters.

Soon the Assad cult started. Just as in Russia the portraits of Marx and the current leaders were evident on every street, so Assad's picture appeared everywhere. Statues of him were erected. No image of any kind was permitted except the pictures of Assad in military uniform or business suits, looking thoughtful or smiling. Assad, and only Assad, everywhere. It was like King Nubechadneser setting up his image and demanding that everybody worship it, or Nero setting up his statue in the Temple of Jerusalem.

Assad had two major aims in life. He wanted above all to be one of the Arab leaders responsible for the final downfall of Israel. He lived in the futile hope that the Islamist regimes would stop squabbling among themselves just long enough to combine their armies in a successful assault on Israel. They tried several times but were never able to succeed. His second great desire was to see Lebanon totally under Syrian control again as it once was. Syria largely promoted the Lebanese Civil War, and Assad didn't care if the country was completely destroyed as long as Syria could be in charge. This desire at least was fulfilled in his lifetime. The Syrians certainly are in control of Lebanon, and the Lebanese are not strong enough to kick them out. When Israel tried to help, the Lebanese people rejoiced and welcomed them as liberators, but the whole World demanded that they retreat.

The Lebanese are in fear of the Syrians and know that to complain against the occupation means spending a few months in jail. Most of the middle and upper class people have left for the United States or France. A standing joke in Lebanon for years goes like this:

A man enters a Lebanese Police Station and tells the sergeant at the desk,

"A Swiss soldier stole my Syrian Watch."

"You're mixed up," says the sergeant. "What you mean is a Syrian soldier stole your Swiss watch."

"O.K." says the man. "You write it any way you want to in the report. Just don't say I said it that way."

Assad tried to act like a Statesman and appear reasonable and intelligent. But in truth he was a brutal dictator who was completely unmerciful towards those he perceived to be his enemies. The following example will show that he was every bit as sick as Saddam Huesein, Idi Amin, or the Sudanese Islamist leaders.

Most of the World has forgotten Assad's brutal destruction of the city of Hamah in western Syria. Hamah was the biblical Hittite city of Hamath, a prosperous modern town with farming and textile industries about two hours' drive south of Aleppo. In February 1982 the "Muslim Brotherhood" began a rebellion there against Assad. Some Ba'ath party officials were killed, and the Sunni Imams called over the Mosque loudspeakers for everyone to rise up against Assad. His answer was swift and terrible. He sent thousands of troops to batter the town to almost nothing and more than 20,000 men, women, and children were killed in the onslaught or executed by firing squad. There was no attempt to separate the rebels from the ordinary townspeople. The city was surrounded so that nobody could get out, and T-62 Tanks under the command of the President's brother Rifaat began unmercifully and indiscriminately to shell the defenseless population day and night. At the same time the population was attacked with poison gas, to teach everyone in Syria a lesson. It is interesting to see the official Syrian website and click on Hammah. According to Syrian propaganda the town (what is left of it) is famous for its ancient water wheels and some lovely gardens. No mention is made of the devastated ruins which can still be seen not far away, and the tours make a desert detour to the water wheels so as not to get too close. Those who are able to get off the tour and go into what was Hamah enter a scene of devastation that looks almost like the surface of the moon. For many blocks where houses, Mosques, and businesses once flourished there is nothing but dust and sand covering ruins that might just as well be a thousand years old. Here and there one sees a part of a rusty car or a child's toy lying in the dust. In some districts a few walls remain showing where a bank or an office building once was. But those walls that do remain are pocked with bullet holes and the streets devastated by shell craters.

Assad was not kind to the Palestinians either. Officially Syria backed the Palestinian insurrection against King Hussein of Jordan in 1970, but Assad as Air Force Chief refused to help the Syrian Army and this gave impetus to Hussein's forces in overcoming the revolution in which up to 40,000 Palestinians were slaughtered. This was known as "Black September" and gave its name to one of the terrorist organizations. It was immediately after this that Assad made his move to take over the Syrian Government. His contempt for the Palestinians was also shown when he had Yasir Arafat and some of his supporters locked up in prison for two months in 1966. Arafat has never forgotten that and hates the Assad family with a vengeance.

Let nobody think for one minute that all Muslims live together in harmony and religious unity. Their rivalry and hatred for each other is one of the main reasons that over one billion Muslims have not been able to wage a successful war against four or five million Jews in Israel. However that will change. One of these days the Islamists will stop their in-family squabbling and turn together against Israel and America. When they do, we may be sure that Syria will try to take a leading role in the attacks.

Bashar Assad is 35 years old, but little seems to be known about him. He was never expected to become a political leader or even a military man in Syria. He studied in England and was trained as an ophthalmologist. One of his major worries has to be that his uncle Rifaat, if anything more vicious than Hafez, will try to unseat him and take over. Knowing that this would happen, his father placed people loyal to

Basher in top military and government posts and they may support him through the first crucial years.

But Basher will have to constantly watch his back with the Sunnis and his own family plotting his downfall. And one thing he almost has to do is unite the country by taking a very harsh stand against Israel. If he could provoke a war with Israel while being guaranteed pan-Arab support, he could well solidify his seat on the throne of the late Hafez-al-Assad.

I wonder if Prince Bashir knows that the Bible predicts his hometown will be destroyed by what sounds like a nuclear weapon and become "a smoking ruin?" Isaiah 17:1 and Jer 49 (23-27)

My taxi almost became a hearse.

Last year I experienced once again the unwarranted and indiscriminate violence of the Islamists against anyone who is not one of their own.

I was returning from the Mount of Olives with several other Americans past the "Old City." We were just about to pass the hill, which many Christians believe to be the site of the crucifixion, when we were stopped by a small traffic jam.

We watched helplessly as a mob of Palestinian youth left the shopping venue of Saladin Street and began to attack the taxi. Our Palestinian driver immediately locked the doors. There was nothing else he could do. The youths started to beat on the roof of the car and several of them tried to turn it over. We were trapped with no way to defend ourselves. A Palestinian policeman standing on the sidewalk watched but took no action.

Fortunately for us the traffic began to move at a very critical juncture and our driver gunned the engine and escaped from the mob.

Until the last few years I had always considered the "Palestinians" to be fairly reasonable people. It is only since our news media have made them out to be victims of Israeli aggression that I have seen a marked difference in their behavior. Only two years ago I would have walked down that street without fear. After that incident I don't even want to go near the area.

CHAPTER 13

The Ayatollah Princes

The Shah of Iran was one of the greatest friends and allies that America and the West ever had in the Middle East. In return for supplying oil to the United States and the "free world" at reasonable prices and for allowing American bases and radar installations to monitor and provide an early warning system against her neighbor Russia, Persia had the blessing of the United States.

Persia, the ancient name of Iran, was overrun by Muslim hordes in 641 as part of their conquest of the "fertile crescent" and most of the known world. It has remained under Moslem domination ever since.

The Shahs were, generally speaking, benevolent monarchs, and the last one gave most of his great wealth to help his people. But this was not good enough for the Muslim religious leaders who wanted total control over the country. They applied ever-increasing pressure on the monarchy and whipped the common people up to a frenzy against their rulers for no real reason. Eventually, the Shah had to protect himself and his government from total anarchy by means of the army and police. The Secret Police (Savac) instituted more and more repressive actions against the instigators of the revolution, which gave the Ayatollahs more ammunition to use against the Shah both domestically and abroad. The Shah appealed to his trusted ally the United States for help in dealing with the situation. President Carter could have sent in the Marines as had been done in the case of the Lebanese civil war and in numerous other countries. But Carter turned his back on an old and trustworthy friend and opened the door for the Ayatollahs to take over Iran and export their venomous brand of rabid totalitarian Islam together with terrorism throughout the Middle East, Europe, and the United States. We will never see an end to the damage caused by Jimmy Carter's treachery. His failure to act has caused the death and imprisonment not only of Iranians but also of a great many Americans and other nationals.

Ayatollah Ruholla Khomeini was born in about 1900 and died in 1989. He was a Shiite Muslim leader with a political agenda and methods akin to those of Hitler. He caused so much trouble in his own country that he had to be banished to France. There, with Saudi oil money, he was able to establish a strong enough political base to influence Jimmy Carter to pull the props from under one of the most stable and friendly regimes in the Middle East and turn the country over to Muslim fanatics.

These lunatics then destroyed the infrastructure of the country, murdered the intelligentsia, turned the women into second class citizens, and turned Iran into the first Islamic dictatorship in modern times. Khomenei preached hatred against the Soviet Union, the United States, and Israel. He arranged the kidnapping of the American hostages and the sacking of the Embassy.

Iran is the driving force and the financial force behind much of the terrorism and war around the world. After his death other Ayatollahs took over and some are even worse than he was. At face value it looks as if a normalization movement is gaining strength and backing a somewhat pro-western President. But we must remember that most of the moderate people have left Iran in the last twenty years, and what is left are mostly ardent Muslims to one degree or another. Therefore, when it comes to taking sides, even the moderates will back the Mullas against Israel and the United States.

A rock through my window

A few years ago, long before this most recent "Intifada" broke out, I was driving between Jerusalem and Hebron in my rental car. I wanted to take pictures of "Solomon's Pools," an ancient reservoir that at one time provided water for Jerusalem and Bethlehem.

As I passed a Muslim village on the hillside to my left a rock crashed through my driver's side window and hit the passenger side door with great force.

Obviously I had done nothing to deserve this attack. I was one of the statistics of people who have been the subject of Islamic Jihad. There was absolutely no reason for such a violent and anonymous act.

Had the rock thrower been more accurate I might well have lost an eye, or indeed I might have been killed. But this is the kind of attack that Israelis have been subjected to for years. Now it is more likely to be bullets than stones.

CHAPTER 14

The Clown Prince of North Africa

Muammar Kadaffi (There are many ways to spell his names.) was born in 1942 in the Sirte Desert of northwestern Libya. His father was an illiterate Bedouin camel-and-goat herder named Mohammed Abdul Salam bin Hamed bin Mohammed, and the birth took place in the family tent about twenty miles from the coastal town of Sirte. Kadaffi's middle name, Abu Meniar, quite appropriately means "father of the knife." His family could not afford nuclear weapons in those days; but the principle remains the same.

The family lived much as their forebears had for thousands of years except that Muammar was privileged to be able to attend school, from the age of ten. For the next four years he studied in the Sirte Elementary School and slept at night in the local mosque, returning home only on weekends and holidays.

As a child Kaddafi was already opposed to the pro-western policies of King Idris and listened to the daily Cairo radio broadcasts of Egyptian revolutionary leader Gamal Abdul Nasser who preached the unification of the Arab World and freedom from the colonials and their puppet kings. Young Muammar memorized Nasser's "Philosophy of the Revolution" which, among other things, described the events that led up to the overthrow of the corrupt King Farouk. Kaddafi began to believe that King Idris could be dethroned by using the very same steps in Libya.

Kadaffi spent much of his school time teaching and encouraging his classmates in his revolutionary ideas and, after graduating, he persuaded some of them to join him in enrolling in the Royal Military Academy in Benghazi, just as Nasser had done in Egypt. A year later in 1964 Kaddafi founded the "Free Officer's Movement" which he again copied exactly from Nasser. Then, in 1969, while the King was overseas for medical treatment, the "Free Officers" instituted a bloodless coup d'etat. The leaders now called themselves the "Revolutionary Command Council," once again copying Nasser to the letter. Soon Kaddafi, with the help of the CIA, emerged as the leader, promoted himself to

Colonel, the highest rank in the Libyan army, and took the position of Commander in Chief of the armed forces, and Head of State. He was the youngest leader in all of the Middle East and North Africa.

Kadaffi now began to pick fights with almost every Arab and African country around him and make threatening noises at the rest of the world. He used his oil money to fund an ever growing army with increasingly more powerful weapons. He planned and bankrolled the 1982 attempt by Palestinians on the life of King Hussein and called the Saudis the "Pigs of the Arab Peninsula."

It is well known that this son of a camel herder has been responsible for countless attempted coups and assassinations. But most of all he is known as the author and sponsor of terrorist activities from the Munich Olympic Massacre to the Beirut Embassy Bombing and the downing of Pan Am Flight 103 over Scotland. President Reagan called him "the Mad Dog of the Middle East." Others have used far stronger terms.

Kadaffi has been paymaster for such diverse groups as "Black September," Abu Nidall's "Fatah Revolutionary Council," "The Irish Republican Army," America's "Black Panthers," and Peru's "Shining Path."

Kadaffi imagines himself as a modern day Saladin, the legendary conquering General of Islam, and as a unifier of the Arab Nation. It is amusing to see how many of these "Princes" want to be the unifier of the "Arab Nation" or the "Islamic Nation," yet none of them wants to cooperate with the other. In fact there has never been any real unity among the Islamists. Each one wants to be in charge. They agree only that they must wage a *jihad* against Israel and the United States.

There have been more than twenty coup attempts and dozens of attempts on Kadaffi's life. He is the sworn enemy not only of the United States and most of Europe, but also of almost every government in the Middle East and Africa. Anwar Sadat stated several times, "He is 100% sick and possessed of the demon." President Nimeri of Sudan said that Kadaffi has a split personality and both of them are evil.

Kadaffi officially lives in a two-story home at Bab Al Aziziya military barracks with his wife Safya and their seven children. However, most of the time he lives alone in a Bedouin tent on a mound of sand brought in from the Libyan Desert. Tethered outside are two camels to remind him of his childhood, and he loves to be photographed praying in the desert.

This is the man Louis Farrakhan looks up to. He is his friend and fellow plotter in the downfall of the United States. In fact Kadaffi has offered Farrakhan one billion dollars to finance the black revolution that Farrakhan plans to use to take over the United States.

For all his socialist revolutionary fanfare during the 70s and 80s, Khaddafi has mellowed with middle age. With his pockmarked, rather boyish face under the military cap showing signs of some serious wrinkles, the bad-boy of North Africa seems to be growing up and learning a few manners. After thirty years of trying to convince the other Islamic Leaders that he should be accepted by them, even if not their leader, he has turned south toward Africa and spread some of his oil fortunes on upturned palms. Not surprisingly this has resulted in a unity of sorts among his African neighbors. On September 9, 1999, twenty African Presidents came to pay homage to the Colonel in Tripoli on the occasion of the thirtieth anniversary of the coup which brought him to power.

For two decades Kadaffi tried to get the Islamic nations of the Middle East to unify into a force which, had they been willing, would have been one to reckon with. But Arabs have always been loners and preferred to be big fishes in goldfish bowls than little fishes in a lake. In particular the other leaders did not like the idea simply because it was suggested to them by Kadaffi, a man they all despised. Now he was trying his charms on the Africans; some of whom were also Islamists.

What the Colonel offered them was a Pan African United States with a central government, courts, parliament bank, and currency. His spokesman said in part, "Our dream is the establishment and the achievement of the United States of Africa. The aim is that countries give up a little bit of their sovereignty in the interests of the whole of Africa."

Tabo Mbeki, President of South Africa, said that Kadaffi's initiative is in line with his own idea of "African Renaissance." But the big question again is "Who will be President? Africans are no better at unity than Arabs and all of them want to be in charge. Kadaffi clearly would not allow that position to go to anyone but himself.

Even so, there is some chance of some sort of unity. Six African nations have agreed to a common currency within the next few years and others may follow. I saw a wonderful photograph of Nelson Mandella kissing the Colonel at the airport at the beginning of the conference. Evidently that is an affair to be closely watched.

Another of Kadaffi's projects is one to bring water from the Saharan aquifer in southern Libya to the coast by building 2000 miles of tunnels. The cost of this is a whopping $25 billion, but Kadaffi is determined to do it. It would be far cheaper and simpler to build desalination plants on the coast for his sparse 5.8 million population. But when the Colonel gets an idea nobody can stop him. By the way some intelligence experts believe that this series of tunnels is actually being built to house the Libyan Army and to store its weapons of mass destruction. But it would seem to be a bit of an overkill to build tunnels the length of the country to do that.

Kadaffi is an eccentric, to say the least. Another of his inventions was unveiled on September 6, 1999, in a Tripoli car park. It was Muammar's first automobile design, and he was very anxious for the world's reporters to see it. They were not allowed to see it up close. They were not permitted to see under the hood. They were not permitted to drive it or even touch it. But they did see it. It was painted dark green, the color of revolution, and it was said to have taken about two years of Kadaffi's time in designing it.

The most unusual part of the design is that it has an elaborate series of sensors which cause it to change shape in the case of a collision (I thought all cars did that) and even rocker panels that sprout wings to stop rollovers. (Ford and Firestone could learn something here). It was said to be the car of the future. Now that sounds to me exactly like the Delorean, or was it the Edsel?

The new car, to be known as "The Rocket," is going into production immediately, or a year or two thereafter, and will be built right in downtown Tripoli so that the inventor can keep a watchful eye on it. Kadaffi plans to build 50,000 rockets a year which will guarantee that in under 100 years every Libyan will be driving a home made green car and cruising through the desert on home pumped gas. Be sure to watch for this new entry in the auto market at your local rocket dealer, Americans.

Speaking of gasoline and oil, Libya sent a delegation to Geneva to speak to a meeting of 400 managers and presidents of the largest oil companies in April 1999. It seems that the Colonel is anxious to bargain with them again about taking some of that surplus oil off his hands at a very good price. The U.N. sanctions imposed on Libya after they refused to give up the Pan Am 103 bombing suspects caused a loss in revenue of more than $26.5 billion, just enough to build those 2000 miles of tunnels.

Col. Kadaffi (or Gadaffi, or Quadhafi, or Qadaffi, or, however you spell his name) has won fame for himself in Libya as a poet and a philosopher as well as an automobile designer and terrorist. He is also an author. His one and only title was the "Green Book." It was modeled, so they say, after Chaiman Mao's Red Book, since green is the color of revolution in North Africa and since Mao already had his red revolution well under way. Kadaffi's little green book outlines his philosopher of the "Third Way," something between Communism and Capitalism in which everybody in Libya lives happily ever after.

Do we still need to be worried about this Clown Prince? I'm afraid so. He has taken delivery of a great amount of Chinese weapons and is also storing other weapons for Saddam Hussein while he is under embargo. He has no chance of fulfilling his dream to be President of Pan Africa or Pan Islam. But he certainly does not want to be remembered as the designer of a green car with wings. He'll be featured in a come-back sooner or later.

Chapter 15

The Chameleon Prince

Yasir Arafat is an enigma—all things to all people. He is at once a terrorist and a statesman; a Muslim, and a Christian; a revolutionary mass murderer, and a Nobel Peace Prize winner; a family man and a homosexual; a dreamer and, above all the embodiment of the Jekyll and Hide syndrome. But one thing is sure; whenever you see him he'll have that stubble on his face and be wearing that kafya draped over his head in the shape of what he calls "Palestine." Anytime that is except when he is off-duty or working in his office. If you saw him there you would not recognize him. Without the kafya his shiny bald head reflects the electric lights. He is no longer the semi-military man in the army jacket. His sleeves are rolled up to reveal his thin, bony arms and he laughs and jokes with his staff and friends. He looks small on television, smaller in real life. His English is really quite good even though he pretends it is not. Above all this man is an actor on the world stage, who perhaps does not really even know himself who he is.

Mohammed Abdel Raouf Arafat al Qudwa al Husseini was born August 4th 1929 in Cairo, or perhaps Jerusalem or Gaza which was then part of Egypt. His birth certificate shows he was born in Cairo, but he insists that he is a Palestinian, not an Egyptian. He says that his mother had left the family home in Cairo in an act of defiance against her husband and that he was actually born among his mother's relatives in Jerusalem. He admits that much of his childhood was spent in Gaza, which was where his father came from, though nobody has any details of this.

He was the fifth child of his parents and his mother died soon after giving birth to a sixth child, when he was only four years old. His father was a successful wholesale merchant with business in Cairo and Jerusalem. His mother was a member of one of Jerusalem's most prominent Arab families. Perhaps that is why he wants so badly to rule Jerusalem. Arafat is very secretive about his early life, possibly because he is trying to cover up the past and forget those early childhood nightmares and disappointments. He is probably ashamed that his mother left her husband at the time of his birth. This was almost unheard of in Arab families as it is even today. There was also the embarrassment of knowing that his father wasted the family's large Bank account and left them almost destitute.

Arafat today is much like that little boy who shuttled back and forth between relatives in Jerusalem, Gaza, and Cairo. He has no home and no real family. He lives in fear, not only of the Israelis, but of his own people. He never sleeps more than two nights in one place. Often he sleeps in the homes of Fatah and PLO members, occasionally in hotels. Wherever he is, one can always see a dozen or so men standing around with apparently nothing to do. They smoke, huddle in small groups, and have their guns ready at a moment's notice. It could well be a scene from the "Godfather" or a similar mob movie of the sixties or seventies. He travels in convoys of fast moving cars with their rear windows shielded and cars carrying gun-toting bodyguards in front and behind. Appointments are made at the very last minute to avoid the possibility of informers passing on details. Food is carefully prepared and tasted before it is given to Arafat. When he flies, he often uses one of Kadaffi's executive jets, available on loan from the Libyan dictator. Flight information is given out at the very last moment and he is treated as a VIP in most airports in the Middle East. Even then he is never really sure of even his closest associates. Much of this fear is probably justified by the number of people who hate him, but some of it also probably comes from his strange and troublesome childhood.

After his mother died, Yasir lived with an uncle in Jerusalem, which was under British rule at the time. As a boy he lived in a mixed society of Jews and Arabs and learned even then to hate the Jews. Returning to Cairo in about 1940 he began to read everything he could about the Jews to "study their mentality," even studying the works of Zionist leader Theodore Hertzl. In 1946 at seventeen, and two years before the State of Israel was founded, he was already helping to stockpile arms in Egypt to smuggle into Israel when the time was right.

When war broke out in 1948 Arafat was among the first students at Cairo University to burn his books to demonstrate that he felt the struggle for Palestine was more important than studying. He slipped into Israel to join the fight, but found that the soldiers of the Arab Legion would not let Palestinians join the fight, and even took away their arms.

After the Arab defeat, Arafat thought of going to school in America, but decided to stay in Cairo University where he majored in Engineering. He trained in the University school for reserve officers (similar to R.O.T.C.) and helped sabotage British installations along the Suez Canal.

At this time Arafat became President of the Palestinian Students League and led discussions about the possibility of taking over Israel and making it into a Palestinian State.

He received his engineering degree in 1956 and took a job with the Kuwait department of public works. Later he opened his own company in Kuwait and became known as a wealthy bachelor who enjoyed fine clothes and fast sports cars. In the late fifties he and some other Palestinians formed an organization dedicated to the liberation of "Palestine" and called it "Fatah." This group eventually came under the umbrella group known as the Palestinian Liberation Organization or P.L.O. and by 1963 running Fatah became Yasir Arafat's full time job.

For several months following the 1967 war Arafat operated behind the Israeli lines but was soon on the run. He escaped over the Jordan dressed as a woman and carrying a baby, an excellent disguise for one who looked so effeminate. This was the first of many miraculous escapes for Yasir, who seemed to have a sixth sense for danger and always found a way to avoid it. It seemed that some great spiritual force was protecting him, perhaps the same spiritual force that protected Hitler, Stalin, Idi Amin, Pol Pot, Kadaffi, and Sadam Hussein.

For forty years Arafat has moved up in Palestinian political circles, surviving coups and attempts on his life as well as temporary political setbacks. He has more enemies among his "friends" than the whole population of Israel yet he survives time after time. He has succeeded by lies and broken promises to convince most of the world that he and his revolutionaries have a right to part of Israel and even a part of the Holy City of Jerusalem as the capital of their anti-God state. They have already convinced the world to force Israel to give them some major Israeli cities such as Hebron, Jericho and Bethlehem and in a Christmas day speech in 1995 Arafat declared "Today Bethlehem, tomorrow Jerusalem."

In a closed door speech to Arab Ambassadors in Stockholm on February 16th 1996, Arafat said the P.L.O. will now concentrate on splitting Israel into two camps Psychologically over the Peace Movement. He also declared that if the Israelis were going to bring Jews in from all over the world, the Palestinians would bring in Arabs and cause a population explosion.

Ever the pragmatist, Arafat seems to know exactly what to say to the rest of the world and what to say to his own people. In the space of one hour he can make a conciliatory speech to the west telling us what we want to hear and then reverse himself when speaking in Arabic to the Palestinians or an Arab council. To the west it is all Peace and Cooperation. To the Arabs it is war and total destruction of Israel.

The private life of the Palestinian Chameleon is perhaps even more secretive than his public life. There has always been a belief that he is a homosexual. Stories abound in the Christian Arab circles of Bethlehem about his boy lovers and his cruelty to them when he has finished using them. Yet there are also stories about women he has supposedly loved including one in Beirut who was murdered by the Christians. He is said to have cried long and loudly when he heard of her death. Most of us have probably forgotten that Arafat was married a few years ago to a much younger woman. Was that a marriage of love or of convenience? Was it a subterfuge to stop the stories of his homosexual affairs? I stayed in a hotel owned by Arafat in Bethlehem a few years ago, the Bethlehem hotel. The PLO men in the lobby were quite obvious and made me feel a little uncomfortable. The discomfort grew worse when I was told that my suite was exactly one floor beneath the suite of Yasir Arafat's mother-in-law. In December of 2000 I felt even more uncomfortable as I sat eating lunch with some American friends in a restaurant in the back streets of Bethlehem. We suddenly began to feel uncomfortable when we realized that this was a PLO hangout. That is probably the last time I will visit Bethlehem.

We shall probably never know the truth about this man. He is the ultimate human chameleon. The one thing we must understand however is what every Muslim in the world understands. We are at war. It is a war to the complete annihilation of one side or the other. There can be no truce. Everything Arafat says or does is based upon that one undeniable fact. For that reason he can quite easily tell Israel and the United States that he wants peace and is ready to make agreements, and at the same time tell his people the very opposite. We need to ignore what he says to us and his speeches to the United Nations, and listen only to what he says to his fellow Islamists. That alone is the truth as far as Yasir Arafat is concerned.

It is interesting to note that while our government shovels money at Arafat and gives him the status of a diplomat and head of state, it really does not trust him. Much has been said about the appalling disappearance of millions of dollars from the funds sent by the United States, the United Nations, and the Europeans. Everybody knows that the so called "Palestinian Authority " takes a large percentage to fill their personal bank accounts, and then cries that there is not enough to feed and educate the poor children in Gaza. What money they do spend on schools goes towards educating the Muslim children in hatred for Israel and the United States.

Edward Walker, former US assistant secretary of State for Middle Eastern Affairs and US Ambassador to Israel said in October 2000 that if Arafat fails to break with Hamas, then a Palestinian State would be nothing more than a "mini-Taliban regime." Walker, who now heads the "Middle East Institute," is very much for Palestinian self-determination. But he said "I have concluded that Arafat will not make peace because he doesn't have a vision to lead his people to peace."

The fact is that Arafat is very much a chameleon caught "between a rock and a hard place." He cannot survive without money. He can't get enough money if he doesn't at least pay lip service to the peace effort. Hamas has him politically by the throat, and Hamas doesn't want peace.

Frankly I see no way out for Arafat or his people except more war and more bloodshed. Hard line Islamists are determined to keep up their terrorism against Israel and their merciless propaganda on radio and in the schools to turn the youth into cannon fodder to somehow destroy Israel. Israel will not be destroyed. When their backs are finally against the wall, they will come out fighting with every weapon at their disposal, and they will win.

Ariel Sharon has proved to be almost as weak a leader as Ehud Barrack and Shimon Peres. Israel will have to return Binyamin Netenyahu to the Prime Minister's Office. He is the only statesman left and the only man who can stand up to all the insanity of the past year and save lives on both sides. The truth is however that both Barrack and Sharon have been forced to abide by the rules set by Washington, and the Saudis as we have seen are apparently blackmailing Washington. Is it not time for Washington to break this cycle and stand up for what is right?

"We are all Martyrs in Paradise."

Arafat's latest statement of December 18th 2001, broadcast several times on PA radio comes on the heels of his recent promises to round up the terrorists.

This is yet another round of double talk from the stubble faced weasel of Ramallah.

How many times will Arafat promise to round up the terrorists for our ears while exhorting his people to more violence out of the other side of his mouth?

The crowd went wild when he said he would gladly give 70 Palestinians for one Israeli life. Apparently they thought that was a good deal. But in my opinion three million of Arafat's terrorists do not equal one Israeli. After all, it is the Palestinians who demand war. Israel desires only peace.

Even so, it seems that Israel is being forced into a war, and that war will explode far beyond the borders of Israel before it's over.

Israel's answer to the above statement was to offer to talk again. Israel will do everything possible to avoid war. But will eventually be forced into one by the Islamists. It cannot be far away.

CHAPTER 16

The Black Prince
(who ate his people)

Idi Amin was a sergeant in the British colonial army in East Africa who rose to the position of Commander-in-Chief after Uganda achieved independence from Britain. In 1971, Amin seized control of the government and elected himself President for Life. He made the announcement of the coup over radio Uganda in these words:

"Fellow countrymen and well-wishers: I address you today at a very important hour in the history of our nation. A short while ago men of the armed forces placed this country in my hands. I am not a politician but a professional soldier. I am therefore a man of few words and I shall, as a result, be brief. Throughout my professional life I have emphasized that the military must support a civilian government that has the support of the people, and I have not changed that position."

Amin then set about destroying all vestiges of law and order and of government. He looted the treasury, sending the proceeds to Swiss Bank Accounts, and instituted a reign of terror similar to the Pol Pot regime in Cambodia. His bloody reign lasted for eight brutal years until a force of Tanzanian troops ousted him in 1979. He is reported to have murdered as many as one and a half million Ugandan people including at least one of his many wives. Eyewitnesses testified that he practiced cannibalism and kept human body parts in a refrigerator for snacks.

Amin became famous on June 27, 1976, when he welcomed the Palestinian hijackers of an Air France jet to Entebbe Airport. The terrorists demanded that Israel release 53 convicted terrorists. The hijackers released the crew and non-Jewish passengers, but kept the 105 Jewish and Israeli hostages and announced a 48-hour deadline to begin executions.

Playing for time the Israeli government announced that it would negotiate with the hijackers, using the time to mount a seemingly impossible rescue attempt which involved the cooperation of several countries, and an incredible plan put together in an amazingly short time. It happened that an Israel construction company had built Entebbe Airport so that the plans were easily accessible. Using these plans the previously released hostages were able to describe the terrorists, their arms, and their habits and provide the force of 200 Israeli commandos with all the information they needed to surround and infiltrate the buildings. During the time the hostages were in the airport, Idi Amin made frequent visits to them, driving up in his black Mercedes with a military escort of two jeeps. He made wild, flamboyant statements to impress everyone of his importance and his sense of justice and almost appeared to be in command of the terrorist unit.

The armada of four Herculees transport aircraft plus two Boeing 707's took off from Israel at 1:20pm on July 3 with Lt. Col. Yonatan Netanyahu, brother of future Prime Minister Bibi Netanyahu, in command. On board were two jeeps and a black Mercedes, exactly like the one belonging to Idi Amin. These were to be used to catch the attention of the hijackers and make them think the dictator was coming to the airport. After a 7-hour, 40-minute flight they arrived at 11.01 pm (local time), exactly one minute past their ETA.

The hostages were freed with astounding speed, with all eight terrorists being killed. On the Israeli side two of the hostages were killed by the terrorists and Yoni Netanyahu died as he helped the hostages toward the waiting aircraft. The dummy runs for the attack showed that it would take one hour. In fact it took exactly 58 minutes proving to the world that the Israelis could do what no other nation would even contemplate.

After being removed from power in 1979, Amin asked several Islamic States to give him asylum. He lived temporarily in several countries including Lybia and Switzerland until the governments let him know that it was time to move on. Finally he came to Saudi Arabia where he was not only welcomed, but also given a pension, a villa with a swimming pool, and a Chevrolet Caprice. I have often wondered how the Saudis who follow strict Halelic rules dealt with Amin's partiality to the occasional human arm or leg. Perhaps they fed him the scraps after a thief's limbs had been severed in the prison courtyard.

Not content with retirement, Amin determined to return to power in Uganda and at one point approached an Italian shipping company to take a quantity of arms to his supporters in Northern Uganda. This proved too much for his hosts. They realized that this man, although an honored Muslim brother, could be a liability if he started another war. He was moved out of his house in Jeddah and given more modest accommodations in Mecca where he could be watched more closely and kept out of trouble. Mecca is of course one of the Harram cities of refuge and he cannot be removed from its confines.

The career of Idi Amin shows that in Islam, anything goes. Many Islamic dictators are well known for mass murder, but few have murdered so many and then eaten them for dinner. Yet such leaders as Col. Khadafy and the Saudi Royal family count this monster as a friend.

Chapter 17

America's Prince Charming

Louis Eugene Walcott was born in the Bronx, New York, in 1933 to parents who had emigrated to the U.S. from the Caribbean. They moved to Roxberry, Massachusetts, where his mother was a domestic worker. His father was a schoolteacher and Baptist preacher. Louis attended St. Cyprian Episcopal Church where he was a choirboy, and he was a student at Boston High School where he was an honor student and track star and excelled in music and drama. He studied later to be a teacher in Winston Salem, North Carolina. He planned to be a violinist and appeared on the Ted Mack "Original Amateur Hour".

In his twenties Walcott earned a good living as a calypso and country music star. At various times he was billed as "Calypso Gene" and "The Charmer," and a charmer he certainly is still. He is to millions "America's Prince Charming." Do princes really turn into ugly green toads? Do ugly green toads sometimes appear to be handsome charming princes?

Walcott's real career began when Malcolm X, the founding minister of the Black Muslim Mosque in Boston, recruited him into the "Nation of Islam."

Malcom X was the chief spokesman for Elijah Mohammed, the son of ex-slave Georgia share croppers. Elijah told a wild story that in 1930 he met Allah incarnate in Detroit. Allah turned out to be Master Wali Farrad Mohammed, alias Wallace Fard. "Allah," was in fact an itinerant peddler who had invented a new Islamic gospel for the black man. Elijah had told some unbelievable stories in his time, but if he could put this one over with the help of this personification of "Allah," he saw a pot of gold at the end of the rainbow. After teaching Elijah the tricks of his trade, Master Wali mysteriously disappeared in 1934 conveniently leaving Elijah Mohammed to take over as his sole representative on earth. There was no longer any real need for Allah, once he had convinced enough people of the basic story and as long as enough people believed that the mantle had been placed upon Elijah's shoulders. The government was never able to prove that Elijah had ordered "Allah" killed, but it certainly was good for his career. Elijah now taught that the black race was created by Allah as his "chosen people," and that the six thousand year supremacy of the "white devils" was about to come to an end.

It was time for the chosen people to wake up, clean up, stand up, and get ready to take over the United States. Elijah Mohammed preached his gospel among the poor blacks, and especially in the prisons, where the new black gospel spread like wildfire. Malcolm X was converted in a state prison in Massachusetts in 1952 and worked his way up in the organization until he was next in line to Elijah Mohammed.

By the time "smiling Gene," "Handsome Prince," Walcott, the country music star, was converted to the new religion, the Black Muslims were well known. They were best known for fighting against everybody including the government and even the civil rights movement, which they said was "just a bigger cage." It was all a matter of power and of who could grab that power first. They set about recruiting all of the criminals, petty thieves, gangsters, pimps, and other misfits they could find. They dressed their converts in suits and bow ties and taught them to greet each other in Arabic. They outlawed alcohol, tobacco, drugs, pork, sports, movies, and television.

Walcott, in a fit of new convert zeal, renounced his "slave name" and became Louis X, imitating his hero Malcolm X. Then, after thinking about that one for a while, he decided that "X" was not dignified enough for a man of such superior intelligence as himself, and really sounded a bit stupid. What he needed was a Muslim sounding name. He didn't like the name Gene or Eugene because they both sounded too "white." He thought Abdul Farrakhan sounded like a mighty fine Muslim name. But he did like "Louis" because that was what his Mother had called him. So he finally decided on Louis Abdul Farrakhan.

Now young Louis had to find a way to make a name for himself and turn this new religion into a money making business. Remembering how well the calypso singing routine and his violin playing had been received, he decided to try writing songs which he hoped would catch on among his Islamic brothers. He wrote and recorded "A White Man's Heaven is a Black Man's Hell." It was of course just a "My wife left me and my hound dog ran away so that's why I'm drinkin' beer in this here bar" kind of country music lyric of its day. But it was dressed in clothes that would appeal to black people. Walcott also wrote two political plays, which were performed in mosques around the country. It wasn't long before black leaders noticed him. It was his plays that made it possible him to meet the man he worshipped and had almost named himself after. Calypso Gene couldn't believe his luck when he was offered the job of assistant to Malcolm X, and a very short time later he found himself minister of the Boston Mosque. He was well on the way to stardom.

But everything in Allah's garden was not coming up roses. Some of the gardeners were unsatisfied with their positions and wanted to move up the ladder of stardom faster than their trainers wanted. Malcolm X staged a palace coup by telling the world about Elijah Mohammed's sexual flings with at least six of his pretty young secretaries. It wasn't that Malcolm was noted for clean living himself, but it was a convenient way to get rid of the old man and take over his position at the top of Allah's Kingdom (U.S.A.) Inc. Farrakhan noted that both he and Elijah taught very strongly against adultery and now here was the Master, Allah's big man in America, breaking the laws he so vehemently enforced in others.

Calypso Gene always knew how to size up a situation for political gain. He saw what Mr. "X" was doing and weighed the possibilities. If he sided with "X" he stood a fair chance of winning. The two of them together could probably topple their chief. But "X" was younger and would be a formidable foe when Farrakhan wanted to make his next move. On the other hand Eligah was old and would soon be looking for a successor. The "Charmer" decided to put his money on Elijah. He thought that with him standing beside the old man and vouching for his purity, "X" would be unable to sway the rank and file of Islamhood.

They would stand behind the Master and he, Farrakhan, would be at the top of the winning ticket. Malcolm X would be the big loser.

As soon as Farrakhan announced his support for Elijah, he was promoted to take Malcolm's place as second in command to the Great One. Not content with his winnings, he staked everything to get rid of Malcolm once and for all. In a fiery and righteous speech, he stated that such a man (as Malcolm) was worthy of death. This *fatwa* set the stage for the assassination of Malcolm X and gave the full encouragement of Allah himself to his killers. Nobody would ever claim that Farrakhan actually said the words "Kill Malcolm X," but that speech from the second highest Muslim cleric in the United States was akin to the Holy Word of Allah himself to the faithful.

Farrakhan was now the acknowledged spokesman for Elijah Mohammed in the place of Malcom X. He proudly introduced Elijah at the next Savior's Day rally held each year on the anniversary of the birth of Master Wali Farrad Mohammed. Farrakhan took Elijah Mohammed's place at rallies around the country when the old man was too sick to travel. He could hardly believe his good luck. Not too many years ago he had been a calypso singer, and now he was wearing the mantle of "Elijah."

When Elijah died in 1975, Farrakhan was dismayed to find that the old man's son, W. Deen Mohammed, wanted to take his father's place. But he knew it wouldn't last. It couldn't last. Louis Abdul Farrakhan was destined to be the head of the Nation of Islam, and nothing would stop him

It wasn't long before Deen made his fatal move. In order to swell the ranks of the organization, he began to insist that the Nation of Islam should invite White Islamists to join. But this was not in Farrakhan's plan at all. He hated Whites almost as much as he hated Jews. After all, hadn't he been preaching that the black race was Allah's new "chosen people?" How would it look if whites were allowed to join? It would make him look like a false prophet. W.Deen Mohammed had to go. And he did.

Farrakhan took a deep breath. He had climbed to the very top of the most powerful black organization in the country. Carried away on a cloud of euphoria, Walcott now set his sights on the takeover of the country by legitimate means if that was at all possible. He was going to be President of the United States. He decided to put aside his hatred of the despised Jesse Jackson and run as his vice presidential running mate. But the two of them proved to be so full of hate, and so anti-Semitic and anti-white, that normal people, both black and white, ran from them.

A black reporter who revealed Jackson's comments about New York being Hymietown and Farrakhan's glorification of Adolph Hitler received another Farrakhan *fatwa*. Nobody was going to stand in the way of this man. Farrakhan called Judaism a "gutter religion" further enhancing his position as leader of American blacks. Pushing the Jews down could only raise the stature of the blacks, at least in their own eyes. In the same speech he reiterated his assertion that American blacks, not Jews, constitute the true Israel, the "chosen people." He made the wild claim that AIDS was a result of an American Government plot to wipe out the population of Africa and that the American Government was pushing drugs into the black community to wipe out the American black population. Of course, it must be remembered that he was playing to the faithful at his rallies and repeating the same nonsense to black converts in the jails, so it doesn't have to make sense. They all yelled wildly in agreement with whatever he said.

Farrakhan now knows that he will never be President of the United States by anything approximating legal means. He lives in his lavish home with his adoring family and gives orders to his troops. In his spare time he likes to play his 200 year old Guardagnini violin and dream of captivating audiences in Carnegie Hall. But he'll never do that either except by force.

In real life he stands on a platform, smiling, benign and wise, in stark contrast to the stern, unsmiling faces of his "Nation of Islam" security forces in their SS style forage caps. He demands reparations for slavery and the freeing of all blacks from American jails no matter what their crime. He advocates an Islamic takeover of America by any means. In his America the white man will be his servant and all will live by Shari'ah Law. Anyone who refuses to convert to Islam will probably be spared as long as he obeys his Muslim leaders and pays a tax to the Islamic government.

Hitler drew his stormtroopers from the prisons of Germany. He gathered his rabble in the face of economic bad times and gave them fancy uniforms to wear. He taught them to be proud of themselves, where there was certainly no reason for pride. He taught them to believe in an insane religion of which he was the high priest. He surrounded himself with these uniformed misfits, trained to kill, and he advanced politically by eliminating his rivals one by one. He used the Jews as a scapegoat and blamed them for all the ills of 1930s Europe and plunged the whole world into the worst war it has ever seen.

Don't be alarmed that Farrakhan is copying Hitler all the way down the line. It could never happen again....... Could it?

In his twenty-six nation tour a few years ago, Farrakhan was promised ONE BILLION DOLLARS by Muammar Quaddafi to bring about the downfall of the United States by mobilizing the black people of America to a revolution. The government said he could not bring the money in, but he already has a large percentage of it. It was reportedly delivered in the form of goods via other countries, which Farrakhan's various business enterprises are selling, but have never been asked to pay for.

In a speech soon after his return from that tour, Farrakhan revealed to the audience that he is the TWELFTH IMAM—the spiritual leader that the Islamic World is waiting for. He claimed to be the latter day savior of the world, sent by Allah to lead black Americans in the destruction of this country, and with it, the destruction of any force for good that America offers to this world.

The Chicago rally and the "Million Man March" were to Farrakhan what Munich and the Nuremberg Rally were to Hitler. The riots of the sixties were a test of what a fledgling organization could do. Now, that fledgling has grown to a fully adult monster preparing to destroy Christians, Jews, other Muslims, and anyone else who will stand in its way.

In November 1998 Farrakhan thumped the pulpit and gestured like his hero Adolph Hitler as he screamed that "We should perform a *Jihad*. The leaders of our government are frightened, and we must frighten them even more."

America is in great peril. Louis Farrakhan is one of the most dangerous men in the world. He is the ultimate racist who wants nothing less than to become the dictator of the United States. Anyone—black or white—who stands in his way will have to be eliminated.

British Prime Minister Neville Chamberlain came back from Munich after his meeting with Hitler in 1938 proclaiming "Peace in our Time." Just a few months later sudden destruction was unleashed upon the world. Two years later America slept through Pearl Harbor. The government had been warned that it was coming but ignored the warnings.

Much worse is coming this time.

Today I took a fresh look at Farrakhan's Nation of Islam web-site "noi.org." I could hardly believe the audacity of the man. "The Honorable Louis Farrakhan" criticizes President Bush for saying so many times "Islam is Peace" because President Bush "is not qualified to represent Islam." So poor George Bush has licked the boots of the Islamist terrorists for nothing. Farrakhan still kicks him in the teeth. Unfortunately I'm afraid that the President will still not have learned his lesson. He probably thinks it is just "America's Prince Charming" who hates him while all the other Muslims love him. Farrakhan's ranting goes on to say that fundamentalist Christians and Muslims only want their communities to return to the purity of the Word of God, and "Islam is a theocracy." We note well the subtlety of this statement. Here Calypso Gene seeks to draw the black churches into his net by putting them on his side and speaking for them. Is "The Charmer" qualified to speak for Black Christians? I can hear many a black Minister exhorting his people to see that "brother Farrakhan only wants a return to the 'Word of God' just as we black Christians do." Half of the Muslims in the United States today are black Americans. How many more will there be after this speech? But the biggest lie of all that the black churches are falling for is that "The Charmer" talks of returning to "the word of God." They don't realize that he talking about the "word of Mohammed."

The "honorable" Calypso Gene goes on to say that America needs a "Day of Atonement as practiced among the Hebrew faith as their holiest day." But his "Day of Atonement" would be for America to worship at the feet of Islam and confess their sins of not turning to Allah.

Farrakhan's "World Press Conference" on "the attack on America" drips with what at first appears to be honey. But upon closer examination in the light of his many threats against America, we can see that it is in fact the venom of poisonous snakes. His goal is to convince America that "Islam is Peace." While George Bush has been told that he is not qualified to represent Islam, The Charmer surely is. Calypso Gene has had his part in shaping Islam for the consumption of Americans. He now casts his net ever wider to catch more and more gullible people, both black and white. The strategy he used to claim that Malcolm X and W. Deen Mohammed were not fit to lead the American Islamic *Jihad* is now being applied to George Bush. But poor George doesn't understand.

The web-site also shows that "The Charmer" is planning a concert with himself as the star. He'll be playing his violin in "A Musical Tribute to Humanity." Well he hasn't played in Carnegie Hall yet. But by the time this book is published, we'll know if CNN has covered the concert live for "Humanity" to see. We'll also know if Colin Powell will attend. Will George Bush send flowers?

Let the bootlicking continue.

Farrakhan will not live forever. But just like the other Islamic leaders around the world, he has another man to step into his place and continue the struggle for the pagan god Allah against the God of the Bible.

The "Nation of Islam" is by no means the only Islamic sect in the United States. I recently met the Imam of one Mosque who is a Saudi Arabian and would have little in common with Farrakhan. There are hundreds of these agents of Islam teaching Muslims to prepare for Jihad. One thing is certain though. When the time comes to strike at the heart of the "Great Satan," they will do it together

And now, as they say, "for something completely different" I invite your attention to the web-site

Fadetoblack.com/farrakhan.

This site provides the unforgettable experience of listening to "Calypso Gene" and "The Charmer," together as always with Louis Abdul and the Farrakhans, singing to a calypso beat. These are purported to be copies of the actual early recordings of the "Star of American Islam." *Warning.* You may not like certain other items on the site – I didn't.

Author's note. While I make fun of Farakhan, I am well aware that he is a superbly intelligent man who has a very serious agenda. I have not said, and will not say, that he has broken the laws of the United States. He has however used his interpretation of the Khoran to manipulate those under him in the "Nation of Islam." They may well have broken U.S. laws in the belief (mistaken or not) that he wanted them to.

CHAPTER 18

The Prince who lived in a Cave

The one who recently ruled Afghanistan and plotted 9/11 is (or was) a dirty, smelly, disgusting little man who is responsible for the murder of several thousand innocent people. He has received far too much publicity, and I do not intend to add to it. It is my hope that he carries out his stated intention of committing suicide. Then we will not have to waste any more money in dragging his case through the courts for the next ten years and giving him a nice prison cell to live in.

He is not worth a page.

May his name be erased.

CHAPTER 19

Islam in America

Most people think they are funny, or strange. The men wear dish towels on their heads and the women dress in a tent with a headscarf or sometimes even in a borqa with nothing showing but their eyes. You see them in the supermarkets and furniture stores of America's big cities and now even in the small towns. But Americans don't fear them. They try to ignore them and they laugh about them behind their backs just as people laughed at Hitler in Munich in 1935.

But the Muslims are far more numerous than the Nazis and far more dangerous. The Nazi weapons were pea-shooters compared to the bombs and rockets that Muslim fanatics are ready to use, right here in America. They've been bringing them in through airports where their own people are security guards. They've been bringing them across the Mexican border in the south and the Canadian border in the north. By now the Muslims in this country probably have enough weapons to destroy every major city in America. Yet most people just laugh at them. Remember they laughed at Hitler and his strutting, goosestepping brownshirts.

As we said, there are well over one billion Muslims in the world today, and over eight million of them are in the United States. In no way do we want to suggest that every Arab, every Iranian, or every Muslim in America is in training to destroy the United States. But it wouldn't take very many. And, once the fanatics begin the takeover, most of the other Muslims will be forced to join them or die, as has been the case in so many other countries around the world. Perhaps you have heard of the barbaric slaughter of Muslims in Algeria over the past year or two. Thousands including women and children have had their throats cut in middle of the night roundups. This is incomprehensible to the western mind, but it is all too common in the Muslim world where terror is used to force whole countries into submission. And it happens here in the United States where whole cities have become almost exclusively Muslim, like Dearborn, Michigan. People die mysteriously or simply disappear.

It is a documented fact that the major planning for many of the Islamic terrorist attacks on Americans around the world took place, not in Beirut or Damascus or Tehran, but in the United States. The headquarters for many of these gangs is now in the United States. The Muslims know that they are in real danger in Cairo or Algiers, but in America it's different. The Immigration Service of the United States will allow most of them in without any real checks, and our police are too busy giving out traffic tickets to notice or care about the Muslim extremists who live here. This may be changing a little since September 11, but most of the damage has already been done.

America is a "free country" with a constitution that allows free speech for anyone, even an enemy. We have unrestricted freedom of movement from one state to another by anyone at any time, even our enemies. And America is one of the two ultimate enemies of Islam that have to be crushed. So what better place for a terrorist headquarters?

The Islamic Terrorist groups have offices in many Islamic countries. Each also has headquarters, training camps, a vast network collecting funds and a large network of spies right here in the United States. They even have a grip on Wall Street. Did you know there is a vast conspiracy of "Islamic Finance"? They have actually pressured many companies to adhere to Shari'ah Law if they want to do business. (More about that in "Ultimate Reich," which will be published in early 2002. Sign up for our email notification on the web-site *DavidJohnsonBooks.com*.)

In the early part of this century Italian Americans were recruited for, and threatened by, the Mafia. They felt that they had no choice but to cooperate. The Mafia's tentacles stretched into every Italian restaurant, every Italian dry cleaning plant, and every Italian home in the big cities of America until they were able to put America into a stranglehold. It took a concerted effort over many years for the police to finally get the Mafia gangsters to a point where today they are almost under control. The same system of threats and persuasion exists today among the eight million plus Islamists of America. There is hardly an Arab here who has not been contacted and reminded that he still has family in Muslim controlled countries. They are all vulnerable to threats, and most have little or no loyalty to the United States.

Thus, Mom and Pop grocery stores become "pigeon drops" for messages between Muslim terror groups in all parts of America. Out of the way farms in Idaho and Nebraska are training camps for Arab terrorists. Middle Eastern restaurants serve as meeting places for terrorist leaders. Telephone calls are made from an anonymous terrorist in Detroit via a three way calling telephone in Indianapolis to a third anonymous terrorist in Los Angeles. The police cannot trace the telephones on either end of the connection because two incoming lines were used. In this way a phone message is conducted using code words between two top members of a terrorist organization. If these details did not come directly from the FBI, it would be hard to believe that such things are going on in peace loving America. But the facts are clear, and they are not being hidden from us. The problem is that most Americans are being lulled to sleep by their televisions.

Television is indeed one of the biggest problems we have in America, in the world in fact. That great scientific breakthrough has taken away our family life, our spare time, and time that should be devoted to God. It has caused people to be captive in their homes instead of getting out and meeting people. It has become our children's baby-sitter, while entertaining them with garbage that we would not have allowed to enter our homes a few years ago, and it has taken over the job of educating adults. But worst of all it has stopped people from thinking. Most Americans watch the mindless soap operas, talk shows, and situation comedies that have not a grain of real humor in them.

Do you remember the time when television closed down at midnight with a prayer, an inspirational message, and the pledge of allegiance. Now, it goes on all night with countless advertisements for psychics, fortunetellers, and 900 sex lines.

I challenge you to turn off the TV and take time to think for yourself. Then go and talk to your neighbors. Invite them for dinner. It could save America.

If a thousand Americans would do that it would turn our country around. If a million did it we could turn the world around.

Someone has to cry out in the wilderness. This Islamic Force is evil and even more sinister than the fortunetellers. Yet the nation is asleep. And worst of all the churches and Synagogues are asleep and the Ministers and Rabbis are asleep. They're waiting for you to wake them up.

> *The only thing necessary for the triumph of evil is for good men to do nothing.*
>
> Edmund Burke

CHAPTER 20

The American Bird

**Is the Eagle still our National Symbol?
Or are we "sitting ducks?"**

In the late 1930's the world watched as Adolph Hitler arrested Jews, Gypsies, Communists, and other undesirables and placed them in concentration camps. The world continued to watch as he formulated a policy for euphanizing old people and the mentally sick. The other world governments did nothing because what happened in the sovereign state of Germany was no business of anybody but the Germans. The world continued to watch as Hitler annexed Austria and the world still did nothing because the new Austrian puppet government set up by the Nazis was in full agreement. Finally, the Nazis invaded Czechoslovakia, but still the world did nothing to stop them because they were afraid of offending Adolph Hitler and Heaven forbid! –starting a war.

Finally in September 1939, when the German army invaded Poland, Britain declared war, but the United States remained asleep. After all the war was thousands of miles away on another continent. So Washington threw some money at it and a few young Americans joined the RAF. It was not until December 7, 1941, when the Japanese attacked Pearl Harbor, more than two years into the European, war that America acted. World War II began with just two countries, Germany and Japan committing aggression and ended only after sixty million people died.

Today, we are faced with a similar threat, but instead of two aggressive nations, we now face more than sixty. While World War II was finally concluded with two atomic bombs, the threat today is from more than a dozen fanatic nations with not only a vast array of nuclear weapons, but also biological and chemical weapons.

Looking back sixty years anyone would say that the threat of Germany and Japan should have been met by force as soon as it was recognized. But instead it was met with appeasement and cowardice. Apparently we learned no lessons because today we are facing a threat from Islam that should have been met with force at least twenty years ago. Instead we have allowed the Islamists to take over country after country and murder millions of innocent people. What is even worse, is that we have allowed them to invade the United States and Europe and grow in numbers until they are a very serious threat to our freedom.

It is difficult to visualize the Muslims as a threat to the world unless we look at a country-by-country report. It doesn't take long to see that over sixty countries are oppressed by Islam and that many of them have weapons of mass destruction. Their power is growing daily.

Should we sit and wait as we did in the late thirties? Or should we act now.

Are we afraid to start a war?

The war is already in progress and has been for years. They started it.

The only real question is, shall we fight back with all the means at our disposal, or should we go to sleep around our televisions and wait for them to come for us?

Please let me know what you think by sending an email via my website

DavidJohnsonBooks.com

There are 6,666 verses in the Khoran.

Is this significant?

Does it have anything in common with

666 ?

Please send me an email.

Tell me what you think.

May I suggest that you tell your friends

About this book.

Shouldn't every American be as well

Informed as you?

DICTIONARY OF ISLAMIC TERMS

Allahu Akbar

"Allah is the Greatest." This statement is made by Muslims during prayer, when they agree with a statement, and also when they slaughter an animal. It has some similarity to the word *Amen*, or the statement *Baruch haShem* (Bless the Name) in Hebrew.

A.H. After Hijrah.

It is the reference used in the Islamic calendar, instead of A.D., which is used in the Christian calendar, or CE for Christian Era in the Jewish Calendar.

Arafat—Plain of

A plain north of Mecca. It is on this plain that humanity will be judged on the Day of Judgment. During the Hajj, on the ninth day of the month of Zhu-l-Hijjah, Muslim pilgrims gather on this plain for one day.

Assalamu Alaikum

A greeting to other Muslims. "Peace be upon you."

Battle of Badr

The first battle between the Muslims and the enemies of Allah. The battle took place between the Muslims and the people of Mecca in 624 and of course the Islamists won.

Barakah

The word means Blessing. Almost exactly the same word as blessing in Hebrew (Barucha).

C.E.

Christian Era. It is used instead of A.D. in Islamic text referring to the dates before the Hijrah.

Caliph

A leader of Islam, Prince.

Dajjal

The Deceiver, a mythological character who changes depending on who is telling the story and which part of the *hadith* is being consulted. In Islamic Eschatology he is the Antichrist or anti-Messiah. He will come forth before the end of time and, after a reign of 40 days, or 40 years (again depending on the Islamic source) he will be destroyed by *Issa*, Jesus, or by the *mahdi*, or both, and the whole world will submit to Allah. Clearly this figure is borrowed very liberally from Christian literature concerning the anti-Christ and easily adapted to Islamic folklore.

Eid

Arabic for festivity, celebration, or feast. There are two major 'Eids; Ramadhan, and the Feast of Sacrifice. The first is celebrated after fasting the month of Ramadhan and takes place on the first day of

Shawwal, the tenth month of the Islamic calendar. The second is the Feast of Sacrifice in memory of Ibrahim (Abraham) sacrificing his son Isma'il (Ishmael). (Of course it was actually Isaac who was offered to God by Abraham and it is at this point that Islam really goes off-track with the Bible). It lasts for four days between the tenth and the thirteenth of Zul-Hijjah, the twelfth month of the lunar calendar.

Emir or Amir.

A prince of leader or some Islamic States. The name came originally from the word for commander.

Fatwa

A legal ruling of Islamic Law. Often this is a death sentence as in the case of Salman Rushdie and others who although born Muslim do not agree with the Islamic faith.

Hadith.

Although the Hadith and Sunnah are used often interchangeably they are sometimes used for different meaning according to Dr.Khalid Alvi in his 1977 publication "Hadith in Islam." We are all, I am sure, very grateful to the good Islamic Doctor for this simple explanation of a difficult comparison. Perhaps his very knowlegable statement can be otherwise summed up by saying that they are always the same except that this is not always the case. He continues by saying that the Hadith means "the words of the Prophet." For those of us who have heard that Muslims believe the Khoran is a collection of the "words of the prophet," it will probably be a mystery without a Columbo, a Poirot, or a Holmes. Please forgive me for being facetious, but I find it a little difficult to be serious about a religion that was invented by an illiterate madman and is now being explained by so many contradictory experts with their degrees and doctorates. In Islam nothing is exactly what it seems, and if it seems to be what it is, it can very easily to changed with the explanation of "interpretation." It seems that the explanation du jour is that since the prophet (Mohammed) was illiterate, he dictated generally what Allah told him and the other prophets have license to explain what he meant as time goes by. It can also be explained by the fact that Mohammed, when asked what was included in his new religion stated that it was a religion that includes prayer and charity. When asked for details he is reported to have told his followers to watch him and do what they see him doing. So Mohammed gave them the headings and they filled in the rest of it.

Hadith Qudsi

The Hadith Qudsi are hadiths in which the Prophet says what Allah said. The meaning of the these hadiths was revealed to the Prophet but he put them in his own words, unlike the Quran which is the actual words of Allah.

Halal

What is lawful and permitted for Muslims. For instance Halal meats are those permitted and slaughtered according to Muslim law.

Harram

A sanctuary copied from the Biblical cities of sanctuary. According to Islam Mecca has been considered a Harram since the time of Abraham even though there is no record of such a place in his time. Medina was also declared a Harram by the Prophet.

Hijrah

The term means leaving the tribe or immigrating to another tribe or country. However in its usual usage it refers to Mohammed's journey from Mecca to Medina. Since this was the pivotal point in the birth of Islam, the year of his hijra is year one of the Muslim calendar.

Imam.

This term is quite confusing because it can be used as a title for many differing positions in the "chain of command" or heirachy of Islam. For example a direct successor to Mohammed, the prayer leader in a Mosque, or the prayer leader when two or more Muslims are together. The term also overlaps with other terms such as mufti, or even a sheik or *sheikh*. Sunni Muslims use Imam for the leader of their Islamic community. The Shia Muslims use this term with emphasis, to refer to one who is considered to be a descendant of Ali. This is because the house of Ali is revered by them as the sacred line designated by Allah to assume leadership. This is perhaps something like the Jewish line of *Cohens* who are descended from Aaron the High Priest and considered a priestly line today. It is also interesting to note that Islam has taken the Christian route here rather than the Jewish as far as the number of worshippers who form a quorum for prayer. In Judaism ten male members over the age of thirteen are required to form a minion , but Jesus said, "Wherever two or three are gathered in my name there I am in the midst." So Islam thought that was "quite nice" and decided that a quorum should be two or more.

Islam

An Arabic word meaning submission. Expanded it means "submission to the will of Allah."

Jihad

An Arabic word meaning "to strive." Some Islamists claim that Jihad does not mean Holy War, which they say does not exist in Islam. In fact they say that the expression Holy War refers only to the Wars of the Crusaders. *The strange thing is that every single time the word Jihad has been used in the last few years it has been a threat made by Islamists against the "infidels." Evidently this is one of the many facts that they need to get straight among themselves. Obviously they are trying to tiptoe through the tulips right now because they don't want Preisdent Bush and Prime Minister Blair to know that they plan to take over their jobs in the next few years. "Let sleeping Infidels lie."*

They also say that Jihad is not a war to force Islam on others, as many people think of it. It should never be interpreted as a way of compulsion of the belief on others which Islam would never do. They point to a verse in the Qur'an that says:"There is no compulsion in religion" Al-Qur'an: Al-Baqarah (2:256). But they forget the other verses in Khoran which tell them to do just that. They also forget the thousands of sermons in Mosques throughout the world calling for Holy War and the forcing of all people to convert to Islam. They also forget (conveniently) Islam's history over 1400 years in which they have murdered millions who refuse to convert. Two million of these murders have occurred during the past ten years but the Islamists would probably say they all committed suicide. Jihad, they go on to say, is not a defensive war only, but a war against any unjust regime. If such a regime exists, a war is to be waged against the leaders, but not against the people of that country. People should be freed from the unjust regimes and influences so that they can freely choose to believe in Allah.

The simple translation of that gobbledygook is that they are justified in attacking any country that does not accept Islam as their only religion and if people get in the way of the Islamic Army, it is not their fault. See the section on two million murders in Sudan in my book "Conspiracy in Mecca" as an example.

Jihad is in fact the struggle to force Allah's Law upon all mankind. Any form of warfare is legitimate when you are warring for Allah. In the case of Saddam Hussein it was even legitimate to wipe out fellow

Islamists (Kurds) in his own country with chemical and biological weapons. In Hafez al Assad's case in Syria it was matter of wiping out an entire city.

So this Jihad, which does not officially exist, soon comes into play when the Islamists find anyone, Muslim or not, getting in their way of total world dictatorship.

Ka'bah

The first house of worship built for mankind. It was built by Adam and rebuilt by Abraham and Isma'il. It is a cube shaped structure in the center of the Grand Mosque in Mecca to which all Muslims pray five times a day. *It was in fact a shrine to the idols of several hundred gods in the time of Mohammed and he simply took it over and incorporated it into his own false religion.*

Kafir

An infidel. One who refuses to submit himself to Allah. *I wonder if our President knows he's one? I wonder if the Pope knows he is?*

Kafya

The headdress worn by Arab males. Yasir Arafat wears one that he says is in the shape of the ficticious country of Palestine. In other words it is in the shape of Israel, the land he plans to rid of Jews.

Khoran

As with so many words transliterated from Arabic there are many ways to spell Khoran in English. I have used this one spelling through out to avoid confusion.

The Khoran is a collection of the sayings and doings of the prophet Mohammed subject to the memories of those who heard and saw them.

It is also subject to changes made by later leaders and interpreters of the intent of the prophet.

Kiswa

The covering over the Ka'bah

Mahdi

The divinely guided one. He will appear at the end of time to combat the *Dajjal,* or antichrist, who will eventually be destroyed by *Issa,* Jesus. Then the *Mahdi* will bring the universal worship of Allah in the form of global Islam. This concept comes from the joint roots of Judaism's messiah and Christianity's second-coming. As in Judaism many men have been hailed as *Messiah,* so in Islam there have been many potential *Mahdis.* But in each case the truth of the office must be proven by attributes and events surrounding the person.

Majlis

Parliament or Council of Elders.

Masjid

A place of worship known in English as a Mosque. In general usage a Masjid can be a formal and freestanding mosque or a room in a house or apartment building used for Muslim prayers.

Mosque

A formal place for Islamic worship. Islamic law states that all Muslim men must attend prayers and a sermon at a Mosque at noon every Friday. Other worship (prayer five times a day) may be accomplished anywhere but should be conducted on a prayer rug.

Mufti

A Muslim scholar or judge. A *Grand Mufti* is the leading Islamic authority in a certain area or city. Sheik.

Mullah

A Muslim cleric. One trained in the Islamic laws. Head of a Mosque.

Mina—Plain of

A large plain within the bounds of the harram (sanctuary) of Mecca, five kilometers from the city. During the Hajj pilgrims spend the night between the eighth and ninth day and continue to Arafat on the ninth day.

Ramadan

A month of fasting for Muslims. It marks the month when the revelations of the Khoran began. Actually they do not fast in the accepted term. They miss breakfast and lunch and spend the evening in a feast.

Shari'ah

Islamic Law as deduced from the Khoran and other writings and added to by sages

The power of the Islamic government is interpreted by the Majlis. The legislators are to make rules and regulations within the scope and dimensions of the Qur'an and the Sunnah of the Prophet (s.a.w.). These rules constitute the Shari'ah.

Sheik.

Master. Headman of a village or Patriach of a Muslim family. A religious leader in Islam. Muezzin. Sometimes the term is used to signify one who is honored.

Shiah

From Shiat or the Party of Ali (see Imam). Islam is divided into two major groups, Sunnah and Shiah. The Shiah follow Ali and his family who feel they have the right to rule as Caliphs in Islam. The sect is further divided between those who believe in only the twelve Imams who directly descended from Ali, and those who believe that all descendants of Ali are Imams.

Sirah

The writings of the companions of the Prophet about him, his personality, his life story. and his ways of handling different situations is called Sirah. The famous collections of the Sirah are At-Tabari, Ibn Ishaq, and Ibn Hisham. The Sirah is a source of reference that Muslims rely on in their daily life situations and problems.

Sunnah

Sunnis are the majority in the great division of Islam. They ignore the claims of the descendants of Ali and take the Khoran and Hadith as their guide.

Torah

The Revelation of Allah to Moses. It is the Jewish Holy Book (Old Testament). *They got that much right. Then they scrapped it and wrote their own version.*

Wahhabis

Another sect of Islam started by Muhammad ibn Abd al Wahhab who preached a very strong message of the unity of Allah. This denomination of Islam is strongest in Qatar where the royal family are adherants.

Zakat

The obligatory charity similar to a tithe of one's earnings.

ABOUT THE AUTHOR

David Earle Johnson has lived in the Middle East and has many friends there. Among his friends are Israelis, Arabs, and Christians and the Arabs include both Christians and Muslims. His research over the past thirty years gives David an insight into the Middle East conflict, which many in our government do not have. It is this insight and personal experience, which will make his books an invaluable tool to help America understand what is happening in this time of crisis. In addition to traveling in the Middle East at least once each year David has lectured in the United States on Islam and the Middle East for the past twenty years.

OTHER BOOKS BY DAVID EARLE JOHNSON

For further information and news of David Earle Johnson's latest books and links to strategic sites which will give you true facts about the Islamic Jihad please refer to the web page *DavidJohnsonBooks.com*

Conspiracy in Mecca, *is the first in the series by David Earle Johnson. Written immediately after the September 11th outrage, it shows how wrong George Bush's statement "Islam is Peace" really is. Conspiracy in Mecca and Princes of Islam together present the full picture of what the Islamic reality is, and how it is affecting the United States and our allies.*

Early in 2002 we expect to be able to offer two new books.

Ultimate Reich, *shows the very precarious position the United States is in and the likely emergence of a world dictator within the next ten years. This book shows how many successive American governments have placed the American people in extreme jeopardy financially and militarily. Clinton's Chinese friends not only financed his re-election campaign but at the same time took the secret information he gave them to place a ring of* nuclear, biological, and chemical weapons around the United States and our allies. A stock market crash is not only likely. It is certain. We cannot survive financially, or militarily, unless action is taken immediately.

Ultimate Reich II, *which will name names and tell secrets about those who will support the world dictator. It will reveal the connection between Nazi Germany and the coming world power.*

0-595-21367-7